The
Emotional Eater's Diet

The
Emotional Eater's Diet

How to understand your emotions
and become a healthy weight for life!

DR PAM SPURR

Contents

ACKNOWLEDGEMENTS

I am so grateful to clients, associates, friends and acquaintances who have shared their personal stories for my book. I'm indebted to their generosity and honesty and have protected their anonymity by changing all their personal details. Their honesty makes it much easier to illustrate occasional points in this book, which is very much about helping people on their personal journeys to develop a better understanding of their emotional life and a positive and happy relationship with food.

A warm acknowledgment goes to my family and friends who have been an enormous support over the months I wrote *The Emotional Eater's Diet*, particularly my brother, Dr Doug Spurr, a medical doctor specialising in emergency room treatment in America, for the helpful nutrition and exercise information.

With special thanks to Fiona Schultz, Alan Whiticker and Emily Carryer at New Holland Publishers for making *The Emotional Eater's Diet* happen.

MEDICAL AND EMOTIONAL HEALTH WARNING

It is important you consult with your doctor or healthcare provider before embarking on any diet or new exercise program. Obviously this is a 'diet' based on understanding and managing your emotions, your emotional relationship with food and getting on top of emotional eating. Hopefully it will stimulate you to become emotionally stronger and also to change your diet in positive and healthy ways.

If you suffer from an eating disorder like anorexia or bulimia you should seek immediate help from an appropriate mental health specialist and/or your healthcare provider. Binge eating disorder is also now recognised by the US Diagnostic and Statistical Manual of Mental Disorders as a type of eating disorder, so if your emotional eating is severe, and you binge, I advise you to check with your healthcare provider for supportive counselling, CBT (Cognitive Behavioural Therapy) and/or other treatments like hypnotherapy.

Such treatment methods you receive from a specialist may or may not be suitable to use in conjunction with this book or other self-help books. This must be checked with your healthcare provider.

My mental health rule of thumb is that if you are in doubt about how serious your condition is then it's essential that you check with your doctor or healthcare provider whether or not a self-help book is suitable for you. I cannot stress this enough.

Although this book is about creating the right circumstances for developing and maintaining a healthy and happy relationship with food, it may contain triggers for someone with an eating disorder. Therefore, please take appropriate guidance from your healthcare provider if you think there may be trigger words that affect you.

CHAPTER 1

The Misconnection Between Your Mind and Mouth

It's your feelings, not food, that is the issue

Welcome to *The Emotional Eater's Diet* (the EED) and the exciting journey you're about to start: a journey all about making positive changes to handling your emotions and, as a consequence, to your relationship with food. You're going to revolutionise your relationship with food and change the way you've allowed emotions to dictate your eating habits. If you have not read my medical and emotional health warning above please do so now.

You may not realise or accept the powerful effect of your emotions on how much and what you eat. You also probably don't realise as yet the power within you to change this situation.

Over these ten chapters I'll explore the far-reaching influence your emotional life has on your eating habits. It will become apparent how, as a consequence of how much you emotionally eat, you may not be a healthy weight. Of course there is variability in the definition of a healthy weight (BMI information near the end of this chapter makes that clear), but generally a healthy weight is one where you feel good, you feel energetic enough to do the things you want to do, and you're meeting your body's needs for fuel.

One of the very first points I must make is that the EED is not about looking like a super-slim supermodel. It is not about being an unhealthy and unnaturally slender weight. It is about your entire wellbeing and improving your emotional outlook and how that affects your eating habits. the EED is about no longer feeling miserable because you seek comfort from food when stressed or challenged by negative emotions. It's about meeting your emotional needs so that you don't try and meet them through food. This will ultimately mean you're less likely to be an unhealthy weight. And you're far more likely to become a healthy weight for life.

UNDERSTANDING YOURSELF BEGINS HERE

I'd like you to ask yourself why you've chosen to read the EED. Your motivation is an important starting point. For instance, do you wonder if this book offers something different for helping you change your weight because you've struggled long and hard with it? Or maybe, do you buy any book with the word 'diet' in its title? Is this because you fear missing out on a new diet that will finally be the magic one that works for you? It might be that you're desperate to finally reach a happy and healthy weight and you've tried so many diets and methods you're hoping the EED will be your lifeline and solution. After all, in any given year about two thirds of people plan to diet and an incredible 20 per cent start a new diet every month.

Here's a truth about dieting for you: dieters don't have success with the majority of these diets because most diets don't meet a dieter's emotional needs. If your emotional needs aren't met you are left wide open to succumbing to emotional eating.

You possibly already know that inner unhappiness has led you to try and 'feed' an emotional hole in your heart. You know there must be a better way to handle unhappy, angry or stressful, emotions that lead you to emotional eating but you just don't know where to start. I expect you're reading the EED for any of these or other reasons.

Let's also play the numbers game—think back over the diet books you've bought or diet articles you've read. How many times have you hoped it will work this time? How many times have you invested money on special ingredients willing this to be the diet to change your life? Thinking through your dieting history might leave you extremely surprised at how much time, money and energy you've invested in dieting. It will help you get in the mindset to make real and important changes if you think about your motivations to diet over the years: unhappiness, frustration, relentless worry about your weight? Yet was there also the feeling that eating 'well' simply wasn't in your control and you were desperate to find the secret to do so in one of these diets?

We're going to get to the heart of the feelings that drive your dieting behaviour and prevent you from successfully reaching a happy and healthy weight. Right now you might be thinking, 'Hang on a minute. I want lots of tips to control my appetite!" Don't worry—there are a vast number of key appetite control tips to come, especially in chapter 9. But also throughout the EED there are numerous techniques to help you understand, manage and control the emotions that help you with appetite control. Most important of all, you'll be helped to understand what makes you tick when it comes to food.

THIS BOOK IS ABOUT YOU

Please keep firmly in mind that my book is far more about the wonderful you than about food. It may be that you do not feel so wonderful, and that's why you emotionally eat. But it all begins with you: you are what is important when it comes to what, when and why you eat what you eat. It's time to stop thinking that food is your enemy—it's not. Although your relationship with food may feel like a battle, it's your feelings that need to be understood, challenged and managed.

I want you to be emotionally energised to the point that you are in control of your relationship with food, rather than having unhappy emotions tempt you to eat food you don't need and may not even want. Please take a moment to recall the last time you ate that extra dessert and felt unhappy, even disgusted with yourself rather than enjoying it. It wasn't enjoyable because it made you feel guilty and even heavier, both in weight and in heart. I'll explain this important emotional eating 'triangle' in coming chapters.

From this moment onwards accept that getting to grips with your feelings will help you find a healthy attitude towards food. You'll be in control of your emotions and they'll no longer be in control of you and your emotional eating.

> *Emotional Eater Energiser: Take a moment (close your eyes if it helps) and hold this thought at the front of your mind: You and your emotional wellbeing are what's important now in changing the way you relate to food.*

YOU ARE WORTH THE LONG TERM

The EED is a diet book unlike others because it focuses on the long term, ensuring you reach a healthy weight and stick to it for your lifetime. You are worth far, far more than the short term. My book is not simply for the bikini season, not only for post-Christmas weight loss, and not just for getting into that special outfit for a big occasion—it's for good, for keeps, forever! Unfortunately, many people who want to lose weight only think short term. They have a goal in mind to aim for like getting into swimwear for their upcoming holiday. But when you think short term you're likely to harm your efforts to reach your desired weight. Dieting research shows that short-term diets lead to more weight gain over the long term.

So short-term diets and complicated long-term diets don't work, but neither does it work when people preach 'sensible living': the 'eat less and exercise more!' brigade. Yes, of course this sounds sensible, and it is, but what these common-sense types fail to recognise is this is almost impossible to do if you're an emotional eater. It's so easy to say, 'eat less and eat better' (plus exercise more), as some experts suggest. But if you get temporary (and it's always temporary) emotional relief from food, it's incredibly difficult to approach food in a healthy way until you understand this 'devil' on your shoulder—the devilish power of negative emotions to drive you to food for comfort.

Common sense means absolutely nothing if you have the best intentions in the world but can't manage your emotions. Because the next time, for example, your feelings are hurt or you're angry and can't express it, you go on automatic food-pilot, comforting yourself by eating.

Then there are the diets that suggest they're for life but often require difficult changes to your life with very strict notions of what you're allowed to eat—high carbs, low carbs, high protein, low protein etc.—whatever the particular diet suggests. How much time do you have to allocate to specialised shopping, specialised ingredients, planning timings and more when you may also have a family, work and/or other responsibilities to think about?

SPECIAL DIETARY NEEDS

Of course, if you have any special dietary needs, for instance if you're gluten-intolerant, you may have to follow a special diet. It's important you follow the advice you've been given by your healthcare professional. You will be able to supplement any important dietary needs with the EED because even if you're on a special diet you may well still be emotionally eating your recommended foods to excess in times of stress.

It may be that you follow a popular eating regime with a high protein intake, such as the paleo diet that many who are not emotional eaters are finding success with.

You may adhere to a complicated method of dieting stating you must fast at particular times or on a specified number of days per week, or a diet stating you can't eat carbohydrates after a certain time. These diets are difficult to follow and even harder to stick to in the long term, especially for those who have busy lives. It may be that the occasional 'fast day' where you only drink, for example, vegetable broths can be good for cleansing your system, but do you want to have to set aside regular days in your already demanding life? From my experience as a life coach helping people manage seemingly unmanageable schedules, I think not.

Instead, as you will see, the EED offers you what you actually need—and must have—to develop a happier, more confident emotional life. That means you'll be able to have a positive relationship with food, and so you meet your food requirements instead of meeting your emotional needs with food.

WHAT OTHER BENEFITS ARE THERE TO THE EMOTIONAL EATER'S DIET?

There are many benefits to following the advice in the EED. For starters, it's all about learning to feel better, good or even great(!) about yourself, to feel capable to handle what life throws at you and the difficult emotions that goes with that. These abilities increase your confidence, helping you stop the emotional eating that's affecting your entire life. I say 'entire life' because I know that inside you probably feel bad about yourself when it comes to fitting into your clothes, being attractive to a partner or potential partner, looking good at work, feeling overweight and unfashionable at social gatherings and so on. Of course there are many other reasons why you would want to be a healthy weight, including the obvious health benefits.

Let's not forget the benefits of living an emotionally happy life in which you're in control of your eating, such as higher levels of energy, as well as far-reaching consequences like faring better in the job market. An eye-opening piece of major research found that overweight women were less likely to get the jobs they wanted and more likely instead to get lower-paid jobs. This is shocking, but unfortunately it's a harsh truth that some people judge your abilities based on attributes like being overweight.

This is a good point to get an honest answer straight from your heart:

* Do you run for the biscuit/cookie tin when you've had your feelings hurt or head to the shop/café/restaurant for some comfort food when your boss has criticised you?
* Do you find difficult or tricky emotions hard to deal with?
* Would you describe yourself as having a problem standing up for yourself, you lack confidence and/or have low self-esteem?
* Do you secretly resent others but find it impossible to tackle them on issues?
* Do you worry that others don't like or respect you?
* Maybe you obsess during a stressful journey home from work about having a snack the minute you get home?
* Do you feel compelled to keep an array of snack food in your home to have handy just in case you're unhappy?
* Does your snacking match your unhappy moods? For instance, if you've had a tough day do you go for a heavy, rich meal of lots of comfort food like meat pies and chips?
* If you've had a tiff with your partner do you gobble up a chocolate bar?
* Are you likely to 'secretly' eat a comfort-food snack when someone has upset you?
* And do you feel unlovable, worthless, ugly, and ugly 'inside'?

I think you get the picture. If you can answer yes to any one of these questions then you probably have some level of difficulty with emotional eating. From today this is going to change. In future chapters you and I will look in depth at emotional eating behaviours and feelings.

THE MISCONNECTION BETWEEN YOUR MIND AND MOUTH

I'd now like to introduce the most important and yet most basic premise of the EED: how some people have a 'misconnection' between their mind and their mouth. Those who have been fortunate enough to be graced with confidence, good eating habits, and a general sense of wellbeing have a healthy connection between their mind and their mouth. They enjoy food socially and they eat food for sustenance. What they don't do is turn to food for emotional reasons. Then there are those people who, for one reason or another, end up with this misconnection between their mind and mouth. They connect eating with their mental state. This means they use the food they put in their mouth to soothe various unhappy feelings, from anger to loneliness and all the emotions in between.

Instead of eating for health and social enjoyment, they end up eating for emotional reasons, and this means they're likely to be an unhealthy weight. Their mouth becomes their point of comfort—when they put something in it that's rich, sweet, savoury or tasty, it helps them switch off from unhappy emotions. But this mind-to-mouth behaviour gives only temporary relief from emotional pain and it's incredibly damaging.

Understanding this misconnection is crucial to developing a happy and healthy way of life and eating. We'll look at this misconnection in more detail at various points in the EED.

MY OWN EXPERIENCE

I went through a time of emotional eating when I developed a misconnection between my mind (and what was going on inside of it) and my mouth. I was expecting my second child and during my pregnancy I almost miscarried a number of times. Whenever miscarriage threatened I was ordered to bed-rest by my doctor to prevent me from losing my unborn child.

It was incredibly stressful as I longed for a second child and the thought of losing my unborn baby was dreadful and frightening. Also during this time it became obvious that my first husband was not behaving as a good husband should. On the one hand I was overjoyed to be looking forward to having my second child, but on the other hand I was despondent over my physical health and the state of my marriage. And despite having loving family and friends, I felt isolated in the unhappiness of my marriage and the fear for my unborn child.

What was the consequence of this whirlwind mixture of happy (at being pregnant) and unhappy emotions? I ate up a storm. I ate desserts like French bakeries were running out of flour. I ate burgers and chips as if the country was going to run out of beef and potatoes. I put on too much weight due to my difficult emotions.

I know what it's like to feel that the only comfort you can get is from a delicious chocolaty, creamy dessert or from a piping hot plate of comfort food even when not actually hungry but when feeling hungry for comfort and love.

Thankfully, a number of things turned around my emotional eating. Not only was I deliriously happy with the eventual safe arrival of my second child, I also opened up about my unhappy marriage to friends and family and received tremendous support from them. Eventually I left that unhappy marriage. My professional knowledge as a psychologist also helped me get on top of my emotional eating. I turned it around and changed it for good. You can too because I'm sharing this knowledge with you.

Even writing about this today brings back the bewildering mix of feelings I felt during that time, so I understand if you're experiencing or have experienced painful feelins that have led to your emotional eating.

Throughout the EED I share real-life experiences with you as it's helpful to see you're not alone, even if someone's story is different to yours. I've changed details like name, age (up or down by a few years), and occupation (to another fairly similar occupation).

Linda's emotional eating experience

Linda, 32, is a buyer's assistant in a department store. When you meet Linda she's friendly, well dressed and you'd expect her to be confident. Underneath that well-presented exterior lurks a lack of confidence and an emotional eater.

Linda has never felt 'good enough' and finds it hard to set boundaries, especially at work. This creates a great deal of stress for her because her boss is demanding and it's a high-pressure environment. Linda took to snacking on chocolate bars and biscuits in the staff toilet whenever she felt stressed. As soon as she munched a few biscuits/chocolate she felt a sense of relief. But that all too temporary relief disappeared even quicker when her boss would make the next demand.

Over three years in her job, Linda piled on an extra ten kilograms through her mind-and-mouth misconnection. Inwardly she knew she should stand up for herself and not let her boss run her ragged. She would practise what to say the next time an overly demanding request was made of her, but the words never came out of her mouth and instead the biscuits went in.

Linda was single and desperately wanted to meet someone but stayed away from singles events, feeling too overweight and undesirable.

Emotional energiser solution: Linda was shocked by the result after I had her keep a food and feelings diary (her food diary analysis to come in chapter 4). She couldn't believe she'd disappear into the toilets between five and eight times a day to munch biscuits/chocolate. The reality of her diary made Linda realise she was in denial about how much emotional eating she was doing and how many times a day she responded to work-related stress in this way.

As well as the diary, to keep her attention firmly focused on her emotional eating I had Linda try the following:

Trigger identification: She thought through the exact types of requests her boss made that caused her personal stress. These were the triggers that sent her running to the toilets to snack. Linda identified three main triggers: when her boss 1) moved forward a deadline; 2) asked her to stay late after work; and 3) had Linda make extra requests on other junior staff.

Trigger specifics: We discussed why these three areas caused her particular stress and how she could handle them. The first (bringing forward a deadline) was a time management issue and Linda feared she simply couldn't meet tight deadlines. The second (staying late) made her feel her personal time didn't matter to her boss, and that added to her feelings of not being good enough. The third (making requests of other staff) made her feel 'bossy' and unlikable to her workmates even though they knew she was simply handing on her boss's requests.

Trigger tips: Linda practised how to say no to a trigger request. The more she practised, the easier her tactful but assertive 'no' responses felt.

Linda challenged her thinking that workmates would find her bossy when she had to make requests of them via her boss. She explored options relating to emotional eating and tried self-reassurance, telling herself she could cope. In self-reassurance she sat calmly at her desk and talked herself out of feeling stressed. She also messaged or phoned a friend to give her a positive emotional connection when feeling pressured by negative emotions. Linda started to move forward as she came to accept that she hadn't been rejected by her boss for setting boundaries. The best news of all was, as she managed her triggers and found she didn't feel like running to the toilets to emotionally eat, she started investigating singles events.

There's a bit of Linda in most of us if we're honest—the part of us that wants to run for cover and emotionally eat to soothe unhappy feelings. But there are far better ways to deal with challenging emotions. Linda's is one of many case studies you'll read that you can learn from. As you'll see, different methods and tips work for different people and situations.

WHAT'S A HEALTHY WEIGHT?

Before we move on to the next chapter, which is about your personality and emotional eating, this section contains important advice about healthy weight from my brother Dr Doug Spurr, a physician specialising in emergency room medicine in the United States.

Unless you have specific nutritional needs or health issues that cause weight gain, here are some guidelines for you to consider, starting with the BMI (Body Mass Index) weight charts that doctors, nutritionists and other healthcare providers use.

BMI is the ratio between your weight and height. It's calculated by dividing your weight in kilograms by your height in meters squared. This gives the ratio that tells your doctor if you are within reasonably healthy weight limits. Your individual circumstances must also be taken into account in deciding whether your BMI is at a healthy level. For instance, there are exceptions for people who have a high BMI that does not reflect unhealthy living, such as muscular people like body builders.

Age	Underweight	Healthy	Overweight	Obese
35+	BMI < 19	BMI 19–26	BMI 27–30	BMI 30+
18-34	BMI < 19	BMI 19–24	BMI 25–30	BMI 30+

WHAT YOU SHOULD HAVE IN YOUR DAILY DIET

Proper nutrition for a balanced diet means that you have the energy to meet the requirements of your day. It'll also diminish the number of unhappy feelings you experience and help you challenge and manage the unhappy feelings you do experience. A balanced diet includes carbohydrates, fats and proteins.

Typical carbohydrates are the different types of sugars, e.g., fructose in fruit and lactose in milk, as well as starches found in cereals, potatoes and breads, and the cellulose or dietary fibre from fruits and vegetables. Typical fats are found in plants, like oils from olives and corn, and the meats and fish we eat. Proteins are found in many foods like milk, eggs and meats, as well as in rice, peas and beans. The key message is that a balanced diet is a varied diet!

Women's dietary requirements:
On average a woman needs about 2000 calories a day. Nowadays you see calories converted into kilojoules, but most of us still relate to the old-fashioned calorie. Women should have no more than 70 grams of fat per day.

These figures are based on an average woman who is active and taking moderate exercise. It should be noted that recently there has been a trend to lower fat allocations for women to 45 grams a day. On a 2000 calorie per day diet that would mean about 20 per cent of those calories (400 calories) should be from fat. However, aiming for between 45 and 70 grams of fat per day is fine.

It is recommended that women eat daily from the main food groups:

* Five portions of fruits and vegetables. These portions can accompany three main meals and provide two snacks.
* Four portions of carbohydrates. In three main meals this may typically include toast or cereal at breakfast, bread or pasta at lunch, and pasta or potatoes at dinner, as well as one of the snacks. For instance a snack may consist of a cereal bar plus a piece of fruit.
* Two portions of protein in three main meals per day. Typical protein portions are one medium or two small pieces of skinless chicken, one medium sized lean chop (cut the big piece of fat off pork chops!) a piece of beef, 60 to 120 grams of fish, 30 to 60 grams of cheese, 50 grams of tofu or one whole egg. It is always better to grill meats and poach eggs

than fry them. Ideally you should not eat beef, lamb, pork or eggs more than twice a week and poultry or fish should be limited to no more than five portions per week.

Men's dietary requirements:

The average man should have about 2500 calories per day with no more than 95 grams of fat. This is also based on an average man who is active and takes moderate exercise. Again bear in mind that there is a recent trend to lower this level of fat to 56 grams per day for men. As noted for women, aiming between these two levels of fat is fine. It is also recommended that men eat the same daily proportions of fruit and vegetables, proteins and carbohydrates from the main food groups, but in larger portions than women.

Dr Doug continues—weight loss is most easily achieved when you're feeling positive about yourself and can simply cut 300–400 calories per day. Making a calorie cut of that amount can be simply done by cutting down on fatty foods and by steaming vegetables rather than frying them. Taking smaller portions generally at mealtimes is also helpful. Following these guidelines, the average person should lose about one kilogram per week until they hit a natural plateau phase a few months into weight loss. This is when weight loss tends to taper off to a lesser but still steady amount.

This moderate method is far preferable to rigorously reducing your calorie intake, as you're likely to experience a rebound in your weight if your body goes into starvation mode. Consult your doctor before starting any weight-loss plan.

When it comes to actually exercising this control to take in fewer calories each day it's important to recognise that your emotional state has a hand to play. As you're reading the EED you will soon become aware of the various ways your emotions affect your eating habits.

Exercise is crucial to your physical health and wellbeing and obviously plays a part in weight loss and management. Don't forget the importance of exercise in keeping you energetic too. Try thinking about the part exercise plays with your weight by thinking about this three-step principle:

1. You take in energy in the form of food.
2. Then you use energy through the use of your muscles.
3. Any excess energy you've taken in that's not given out through exercise will be stored as fat. The happier and more positive you become, the less likely you'll take in excess energy in the form of excess food.

Once you're on track you should aim for four sessions of twenty minutes each per week of aerobic exercise. Alternatively, a mere fifteen minutes of exercise daily has been shown to increase your lifespan by three years.

Aerobic exercise is any exercise that increases your heart rate. Good and accessible examples are swimming, cycling, jogging, brisk walking, and even a brisk walk with your dog. It's important to also stretch out your muscle groups during the week, ideally aiming for ten minutes per day. Gentle stretching and yoga-type exercises should be done without 'bouncing', which can injure muscles.

Always make sure any stretching is done when you're in a secure position with good footing so you don't injure yourself. Yoga classes are ideal for learning to stretch properly and as an introduction to an exercise programme.

Regular exercise and stretching out your muscle groups generally ensures that your muscles and bones stay strong and flexible and also improves your heart rate and circulation. This has the added benefit of releasing endorphins—the natural, so-called feel-good hormones. I provide additional energising, metabolism-boosting advice in chapter 8.

Ultimately what we're aiming for with the EED is for you to reach a weight where you are healthy and well, your energy needs are being met, you're satisfied with your size and crucially you're eating for health and sociability and not for emotional reasons.

At time of going to print there had been suggestions that the BMI should be revised but as yet the suggested changes haven't been adopted by the NHS (UK).

As an alternative to BMI the World Cancer Research Fund's nutritionist recommends the healthy waistline dimensional as one guide to healthy weight.

They advise the following:

1. Place a tape measure around your waist at the halfway point between the bottom of your lowest rib and the top of your hipbone. This is the point at which to measure your waist.
2. Make sure the tape is straight and snug but doesn't compress your skin.
3. Measure after breathing out.

What is a healthy measurement?

As a guide, a healthy waist measurement is:

* less than 31.5"/80cm for women
* less than 37"/94cm for white and black men
* less than 35"/90cm for Asian men

This may seem easier to achieve when younger, but it is important that we all try to be as lean as possible around the waist at any age.

On to chapter 2, where I'll take a closer look at your personality and how it relates to emotional eating.

Personality and Emotional Eating

Your personality traits weave together to make the person you are, including your emotional eating

We're going to take a look at how your personality traits relate to your emotional eating. These traits from childhood onwards connect to the early development of your relationship with food.

Many people worry that their personality is their personality for life and they're stuck with it despite feeling unhappy with how they view themselves. However, while personality traits are usually relatively stable, they aren't necessarily set in stone. With understanding, you can enhance the traits that will make a difference to your emotional eating. For instance, you might have had a difficult start in life with neglectful parents that left you with a deeply insecure personality. But then thankfully you found unconditional love in your foster family and you developed a more secure personality.

Equally, though you might have been a happy child everyone viewed as having a confident personality, then something happened in your life to make you lose that natural confidence (e.g., parents' divorce). Along with that confidence went the feeling that you could discuss life's hurdles and instead you chose to eat to soothe difficult emotions.

Both these positive and negative examples show that certain traits can evolve one way or another with the events of our lives. Let's work on understanding the personality traits that might hold you back and strengthen those that'll help you move forward.

NATURE VERSUS NURTURE

You have probably heard of the 'nature versus nurture' debate on personality—'nature' being how much of your personality is genetic and inherited, 'nurture' being how you were treated by your parents, and as you grew older how you were treated by extended family, friends or teachers and what effect this had on your developing personality.

Both nature and nurture are important, but we're going to focus on traits that emotional eaters need to be aware of, beginning with how your eating habits may have been influenced by your parents' personalities and the impact they had on your developing personality.

THE IMPACT OF YOUR PARENTS

Don't underestimate how your parents' personalities have influenced the development of yours, including behaviour like emotional eating. We all have different sides to our personalities. We certainly present a different side of ourselves at work, and we hope that at home is where we feel secure enough to be our true selves. Though as we'll see with some case studies whether you are able to be yourself at home depends on how you're treated by your parents.

Certainly at home is where we witness the positive and negative traits in our parents' personalities. For instance, if you had an arrogant father and a timid mother you may well end up with an arrogant or a timid streak to your personality. If you had an outgoing, 'life and soul of the party' mother and a shy father, one of these traits—shy or outgoing—might be dominant in your personality.

These traits relate to all our behaviour, including our eating habits. Emma's story is a good example of this.

Emma's emotional eating experience

Emma, a nurse, is a 41-year-old divorced mother of two who's been an emotional eater for as long as she can remember. Her father was a shy computer programmer and her mother the opposite—a very outgoing personality who threw lots of parties.

Emma recalls being happiest at her father's side. She loved the quiet, and only in our discussions realised that his shy quiet side was much more of her natural personality. However, her mother always insisted on Emma helping at her various functions from a very young age. Her mother would wheel Emma out to anything from a summer barbecue to a Christmas drinks party and expect Emma to shine. Essentially, her mother tried to shape Emma's quieter personality to be more like her own.

From about age five Emma describes herself as 'tubby'. This was because the pressure on her from her mother to shine socially meant she was always snacking. Emma vividly recalls carrying plates of food off to the corner to wolf down at her mother's parties. The pretence of having an outgoing personality continued.

Pretending to have an outgoing personality as a naturally shy person is incredibly stressful and Emma realised that this contributed to the breakdown of her marriage. Her ex-husband was very sociable and although in their early years Emma pretended she was outgoing too, they ended up constantly arguing about how much they socialised.

Despite the divorce, Emma still displayed a very different personality at work to who she really was. We discussed how all of us put on a façade in the workplace, but that's very different to always pretending to be an outgoing person when clearly you're not. Such extreme personal stress clearly drove Emma to emotional eating.

Emma also worried she was pressurising her own daughters to be more outgoing. Inwardly she knew she shouldn't repeat her mother's behaviour. But on the other hand she didn't want them to feel shy inside the way she did.

Emotional energiser solution: As you can see, and as Emma accepted, trying to shape a child's personality in opposition to where they naturally fall, for example, on a scale of shy to outgoing, was already repeating itself in Emma's family.

Trigger identification: With a careful study of her food and feelings diary Emma discovered her emotional eating was largely triggered by 1) being asked to present something at work, for instance a new nursing procedure and also 2) when fellow staff members asked her to socialise after work.

Trigger specifics: Emma felt these two areas caused her particular emotional stress as she had to put on a social performance that completely went against the grain of her natural personality. This was particularly true when asked to present to her colleagues, which made her anxious. Emma was a particularly proficient nurse and was often asked to demonstrate new techniques and procedures. Inside, she feared the 'real' Emma was going to be discovered and she felt the real her wouldn't be well liked or would be ignored by others.

Trigger tips: It was crucial that Emma learned to relax in these situations because they happened frequently. Using a Dictaphone, we recorded a mini relaxation tape specifically tailored to her needs. Emma was to listen to this daily and whenever she needed it, as there were two versions, a three-minute pep talk and a fifteen-minute version for the evening.

Self-challenging: Emma needed to challenge her panicky thoughts when she was asked to present a procedure. I asked her to visualise her most recent success when she had presented something and felt good about it. She was to hold this success at the front of her mind any time she had to present or socialise when she didn't want to, and challenge her anxious feelings.

Shopping awareness: Emma's food diary showed quite clearly if she was stressed about having to pretend to be confident, that was when she'd shop and buy her favourite comfort foods. Instead she was to stop herself, calm down, listen to her pep-talk tape, and telephone a friend for reassurance if it got to that point.

Revealing her true self: A crucial step forward was for Emma to start revealing the real her one step at a time at work and social gatherings. Before each presentation or gathering she reassured herself that she didn't have to go in and be one of the most outgoing. If she felt in a quiet mood or she didn't have anything to say beyond the presentation, then she was going to accept that and not worry about it. This was to be practised daily in any anxiety-provoking social situation.

Emma also sought treatment for depression from a specialist—a wise decision. This specialist treatment, coupled with EED coaching from me, helped her gain control of her emotional eating and improve many aspects of her life.

You might find there's a link to depression in your emotional eating. Especially if this behaviour has been going on since childhood, as with Emma, it's highly likely you've felt deeply unhappy, even chronically depressed about it. One leading psychiatrist in this area, Professor Christopher Fairburn of Oxford University, has found depression in many emotional and binge eaters. Please speak to your doctor if you are concerned about depression.

You may already have considered that something as serious as depression may underlie your emotional eating, or it may cause you some anxiety to even think along these lines. A rule to live by is that facing what makes you anxious means gaining control of it. Control will lead to much greater confidence and a new, confident, in-control you.

ASPECTS OF PERSONALITY AND YOUR EMOTIONAL EATING

There are various theories of personality, but as this is a self-help book and not a psychology textbook I'll focus on three key aspects I think are particularly relevant to your emotional eating: 1) confidence versus lack of confidence; 2) outgoing/extrovert versus shy/introvert; 3) impulsivity versus control.

Because the 'misconnection' between your mind and mouth has a lot to do with your individual traits, let's go through them one at a time so you can think about how they apply to you.

Confidence/security versus lack of confidence/insecurity

This personality trait is relevant to so many aspects of your wellbeing, as well as your emotional eating. Confidence is associated with so many positive qualities including feeling good enough about yourself to express your emotions, to set your boundaries and to know your own mind. All of these qualities relate to emotional eating. You only have to think of Linda and Emma's stories and how a lack of confidence meant they weren't the 'mistress of their emotions', leading to emotional eating.

Confidence is not to be confused with arrogance. Unfortunately many goodhearted people think they'll look arrogant if they express themselves. You won't! The arrogant person pushes their way through life without considering others. The confident person knows their own mind, is open-minded when they don't know their own mind, and respects other people's opinions and feelings.

How about you? How confident are you? Take this mini-quiz as a quick gauge. Only honest answers will do.

1. You speak out at a work meeting and someone immediately gives a different point of view:

A. Wish the ground would swallow you up and think that teaches you for opening your mouth.

B. Feel a bit daunted but enter a discussion with them on your different points of view.

C. Don't take it at all personally and get on with a good, helpful discussion.

2. **You're single and see someone attractive:**
A. You don't dare look in their direction.
B. You occasionally glance at them hoping they're looking at you.
C. You go speak to them or give them clear signals to come speak to you.

3. **Within your family you always felt:**
A. You and your feelings were overlooked.
B. You wished for more attention at times.
C. You were treated equally.

4. **You've bought something that's faulty or have had bad service:**
A. Fret a lot about it but don't return it or say anything.
B. Have to really 'talk yourself up' to do something about it.
C. Have no problem returning the item or commenting about the bad service.

5. **The host/hostess is insisting you have seconds of the dinner you complimented that they cooked:**
A. Despite being overly full you say yes.
B. You feel you have to say yes but only to a small portion of seconds.
C. You say again how delicious it was but you simply can't manage anymore.

6. **A friend/work colleague/family member repeatedly asks for favours, some of which are hard for you to carry out:**
A. Feel very stressed about it but think you can't say anything.
B. Worry about rocking the boat but occasionally say no to doing a favour.
C. Are completely able to say no when you can't do a favour.

Three or more As and the rest Bs: Low confidence

This indicates you may have low confidence that probably plays a part in your emotional eating. Confidence is crucial in preventing emotional eating. The higher your confidence, the more likely you are to face your emotions, manage tricky situations without fear of rejection and know in your heart that while you look after your own needs you won't ignore the needs of others.

Start using these tips today to boost your confidence:

* Dare to start believing that you have a right to be treated well.
* Challenge negative thinking like, 'I'm useless!' and change it to, 'I've got loads of qualities!' Challenging negatives should become a habit.
* Develop a 'cup half full' attitude, focusing on the positives in your day.
* Don't live by regrets like, 'Why didn't I do X or say X, Y or Z?. Live in the real world, making the most of what you've got and move forward from regret.
* Emphasise your best attributes—remind yourself daily that, for example, you're a great friend, you're thoughtful, you have a good sense of humour.
* Accept that people won't reject you if you stand up for yourself.
* Think through what you plan to say, for example, when taking back a faulty item, complaining about service or setting boundaries on how much food you eat, and imagine a positive outcome.

Three or more Bs and no more than one A: Moderate confidence

It's great you appear to have moderate confidence but if other factors are at play causing you emotional upset then your confidence may not protect against emotional eating. Follow the above points as well as:

* Think through the situations where your confidence is high. What do you do in those situations that you can bring to

when your confidence is challenged?
* Use 'feel-good' tricks like playing music that lifts you or visualising a happy memory when feeling negative.
* Definitely trust your intuition, as it's working some of the time. So be cautious when self-doubt creeps in over decisions that you make.
* Develop a new skill that'll help create a new frame of mind. Plan manageable steps to reach this goal.
* Think about any question you gave an A answer to. How can you work on that specific area to gain more confidence?
* Accept that things don't always go to plan, no one always feels confident, and the mistakes and so-called failures of life are there to learn from.

Four or more Cs and no As: High confidence

It seems you've got solid confidence, but even a confident person can emotionally eat when things get tough. Keep your confidence high:
* Make a point of encouraging others so that your confidence spreads to them.
* Keep learning from how well you handle a variety of situations.
* Read through the tips above, because even a confident person can benefit from advice.

Make a note here of something you could do today to start boosting your confidence:

_____

_____

_____

_____

_____

_____

_____

_____

OUTGOING/EXTROVERT VERSUS SHYER/INTROVERT

We all have a good idea of what we mean by an outgoing extrovert compared to a quieter or shyer introvert. When we talk about someone being the life and soul of the party we think of someone who can let go, be themselves and enjoy the moment. We make equally big assumptions about a quieter person—that they're insecure, don't have a lot to say for themselves, can't let go, can't relax and other negative traits.

Of course these are sweeping generalisations—the outgoing extrovert may actually be a selfish bore who doesn't think about involving other people. The introvert may actually be far more interesting given half the chance, as well as being surprisingly confident.

So don't be fooled that all extroverts are happy, confident, fun people as some are actually overcompensating; their lively, loud, party-person personality may be a front for shyness. Some are unhappy inside and try desperately hard to appear outgoing. I've met as many so-called extroverts as so-called introverts who are unhappy emotional eaters.

How extroverted or introverted are you? Answer this checklist honestly:

1.	Shyness holds me back	YES	NO
2.	I don't enjoy social gatherings	YES	NO
3.	It takes me time to open up to others	YES	NO
4.	I hate being asked to, e.g., give a presentation	YES	NO
5.	Sometimes people try to bring me out of my shell	YES	NO
6.	I've never been told I'm too loud	YES	NO
7.	I prefer being at home than out in a group	YES	NO
8.	I don't like being the centre of attention	YES	NO

Mainly yes answers suggest you're more of an introvert, and mainly no answers suggest you're more of an extrovert.

At an anecdotal level from people I've met personally and professionally, I find you may well have emotional eating difficulties being at either end of this trait—it often depends on how well you communicate despite being, for example, a quieter person. If you communicate well it is often easier to manage difficult emotions.

Introverts and emotional eating

Why is emotional eating sometimes a problem for the quieter, shyer, more inhibited introverts? Because there can be a longing to break free from this aspect of your personality. Inwardly you may feel quite restricted by being an 'introvert', especially because of the way people react to you. The assumptions they make about you can make you feel negatively about yourself.

How does this relate to emotional eating? When facing any emotional difficulty, if you feel you have to manage it on your own, as many introverts do, it can overwhelm you. Opening up to others when you need to, for instance over a work issue, may seem daunting. But fretting inside about a situation can lead you to the comfort food cupboard.

As a potential introvert (I say 'potential' because above is only a mini-checklist) start making small changes:

* If you have an opinion on a new film, TV programme, some music you've heard, get the courage to express yourself
* Make a point of expressing your opinion on something every day. Once you realise the world won't fall down on your head because you've given an opinion, it becomes easier to start speaking up on the bigger stuff.
* When speaking up about an issue, start by mentioning something positive. Let's say you're unhappy with how much your partner goes out. Raise the topic by highlighting the fun you two had when you did something together recently. Then take it to the next level and say you wished you could share more times like that and that they'd go out less with their friends.

Extroverts and emotional eating

For the bolder, louder extroverts, why might you emotionally eat? As I mentioned, one main reason is because of the pressure to be entertaining and to be the one people count on to get a party started or to make a work event more exciting. This can be a lot of pressure, especially if you're pretending to be something you're not.

As a potential extrovert it's time to start allowing yourself a more relaxed approach to life:

* Stop yourself when you know you're about to take over the conversation.
* Listen to others and respond to what they have to say.
* Have fun but don't feel you have to take over, for example at a party.
* Let your guard down and let people know if you're not in a particularly loud party-person mood. You're not going to be rejected, and if you were it'd only be by shallow people who want to be entertained. And that tells me they may see you more as a court jester.

Does anything ring true to you about introversion versus extroversion? Write down any discovery about yourself here:

_____

_____

_____

_____

_____

_____

_____

_____

_____

_____

_____

_____

_____

_____

IMPULSIVE VERSUS SELF-CONTROLLED

This aspect of personality is all about how much you act on impulse in responding to your environment. People range from those who act immediately, or who need/want instant gratification, to those who exercise self-control in their reactions. This aspect of personality has a vital role in emotional eating.

Those who act impulsively and without thought often regret their actions. Regret surfaces when they've acted impulsively on something as big as breaking up with a partner, or spending too much while shopping, or smaller things like flying off the handle. The impulsive person then feels guilt for their actions and a natural response to such challenging emotions is emotional eating. If an impulsive person is craving emotional comfort they're often likely, on impulse, to head for comfort food. They literally don't think about it. Is this you? Do you find yourself in one moment under stress and the next moment eating, while barely noticing?

How about if you're the opposite and over controlled? This is not to be confused with the introvert who wishes at times they had a freer, more open personality. You might be outgoing and far from shy but as an over-controlled personality you try to keep a tight lid on things and keep your life nice and orderly. Sometimes this is over-compensation for anxiety. And if you're overcompensating for difficult, anxious feelings then you're at risk of being like an emotional pressure cooker. You let things build to a flashpoint and then unleash what appears to be impulsive behaviour (like the people on the opposite end of this trait to you!) such as bingeing on comfort foods—in other words, emotional eating to excess.

When the over-controlled person unleashes their unhappy emotions they also regret it. Then the same cycle of regret and guilt starts over again. And how do you comfort this? If you struggle with emotions for whatever reason then you comfort this with more emotional eating.

This is the triangle of emotional eating: You feel unhappy for whatever reason, you act on this emotional unhappiness with emotional eating, you then feel guilt and regret for doing so . . . and so the triangle starts all over again.

The Triangle of Emotional Eating

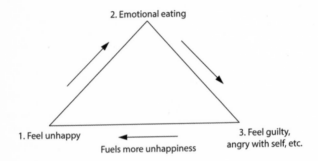

Take this quick quiz, answering questions honestly (as always!):

1. Do you see things in the shop and buy them without thinking?
A. No, I'd never make an impulse purchase.
B. Sometimes I buy without thinking.
C. I frequently buy things and regret it.

2. Do you dive headfirst into relationships?
A. No, I always take my time.
B. Once or twice I've gone into a relationship without thinking.
C. I always dive into relationships.

3. Do you ever realise you've eaten something only after you finished it?

A. No, that's never happened to me.

B. Occasionally I'll eat something when I'm only half aware of it.

C. I'm always finding I've eaten something without realising it till it's finished.

4. Do you say things that you immediately regret?

A. No or very rarely.

B. Sometimes I do.

C. All the time.

5. Do you take up and then give up hobbies, interests or projects quickly?

A. No, I think about something before I take it up and then stick with it.

B. A few times.

C. I constantly do this.

Three or more Cs and no more than one A: High impulse/low control

Your answers suggest you may be high on the impulsivity aspect of personality. There's much you can do to manage this side of your personality to help you come to grips with the emotional eating that may go hand in hand with it.

Each day try these:

* Become aware of impulses as they build. Sometimes a person senses that certain behaviours are about to burst forth but they ignore it—don't. Think before you act.
* Take a moment to sit back and consider the building impulse. How could you handle it?
* If you don't already, definitely take up physical exercise to take the edge off any excess energy you might have (more on fun exercise in chapter 8).

* Be especially aware when shopping for food that you don't just snatch snack food and put it in your trolley.
* Pause before you go to the checkout and look at every item in your basket. Are they healthy choices? Do you need to put some of these things back?

Developing your willpower further: Other strategies to develop your willpower include:
* Counting to ten before you say something you might regret.
* Rereading emails/texts/messages that contain any potential issues in them before you send them.
* Send them to yourself and read them as if you just received them from someone else.
* Your food and feelings diary in chapter 4 will help you identify your specific triggers. But in the meantime try replacing the impulsive hand-to-mouth eating behaviour that you don't realise you're doing. Keep snack foods away from your desk during work and out of the TV room when you're watching TV at night.
* Buy worry beads to soothe hands that are used to hand-to-mouth movements.

Automatic food-pilot: You might find you go on automatic food-pilot, comforting yourself by eating, especially if you're impulsive by nature. This is when those hand-to-mouth behaviours kick in and you automatically start eating. One personality trait that'll help you counterbalance this automatic food pilot and will positively benefit your progress with the EED is patience. The strategies above to help develop patience will benefit you, but also try these:
* You always open your birthday presents first thing on your birthday. Put that off and open them at lunchtime or dinner. Try doing this with Christmas and any other holiday, delaying your desire for instant gratification.
* You're waiting for a text/email/message and you keep checking your phone or laptop. Again, put a time limit on this to wait thirty

minutes, to an hour and longer before you check again.

* Develop patience when you're expecting to have a delicious dessert after dinner. Leave at least a twenty-minute gap before enjoying that dessert. The same idea applies to thinking you need a snack—have a glass of water and delay at least thirty minutes before you have one.

* Set the alarm on your phone or use an egg timer to help train yourself to get used to these 'pause-times', where you pause before eating or acting on impulse.

Patience pays off with weight loss: A major study found that the long-held belief that cutting down 500 calories per day will result in losing one to two pounds a week now seems to be slightly misguided. Instead, as mentioned in the introductory chapter, weight loss has been found to slow down over a number of months. However, you will still continue to lose weight with healthy eating, exercise and, from my perspective, as you address any emotional eating habits.

Those with natural patience are more likely to see this through and continue a slow but steady weight loss. Those who are impatient—perhaps having an impulsive streak—give up when they plateau rather than seeing it through. Increase your patient side to grow stronger.

Three or more Bs and no more than one C: Balance between impulse and control

Your personality may strike a balance between impulsivity and over-control, however it never hurts to look at the advice for those who are more impulsive (above) and those who are more over-controlled (below).

Three or more As and no more than one C: Low impulse/high control

Your high levels of self-control will have many benefits. The

41

problems start when you're so over-controlled you don't face challenging emotions. These have to come out at some point and that's when you may emotionally eat.

Overcoming the over-controlling side of your personality: First, explore where your controlling ways come from. Maybe your mother and/or father were controlling so this became part of your personality and your way of dealing with the world. Perhaps after an unhappy event like going through a divorce you started to feel the need to control an uncertain world and this became ingrained in your nature? Think about this carefully to understand this trait better. Here are some steps to take:

* Self-reassurance. Start reassuring yourself that it's okay to let go occasionally. Introduce a soothing strand to your normal thinking which is probably always about keeping on track, taking control and doing the right thing. Tell yourself it's okay to slow your pace and not juggle too many balls.

* Be mindful of your emotional state. Those who score high on the trait of being over-controlled often ignore it. You put yourself at risk of the pressure-cooker effect and resulting emotional eating.

* Sometimes the little things make a big difference to changing your need to control everything. Change a small part of your routine daily, for example, try a new café at your lunch-break, shop somewhere different, go for drinks with a colleague at a new place. Appreciate these little experiences.

* Test the waters by relaxing over slightly bigger things you normally fret over. Select an area that's not a major priority to test. For instance, maybe your partner's a reasonable cook but you still badger them to prepare food your way. Don't enter the kitchen when they're cooking. Do something unrelated, like relaxing in a soothing bath. By removing yourself and then appreciating what they've done, it's a test of your feelings about this area of control. Hopefully you'll like

this sense of letting go. Do these tests at least weekly.

* Now throw caution to the wind and select something you value highly and always control, say, booking a holiday or planning a group presentation at work. Let someone else do the lion's share and give up responsibility for this. Resist checking-up to see how they're managing the task and enjoy the extra time this frees up for you.

Self-control is like working out a muscle

Psychologist Roy F. Baumeister suggests thinking of self-control as like a muscle—when it's 'worked-out' it can be temporarily depleted. In other words you exercise control, then in another situation again exercise control, and then yet again you exercise self-control, but then you might end up thinking, 'I can't be bothered, I'm just going to go for it' (in this case 'it' being the foods that satisfy your emotional cravings), and self-control goes out the window.

I think this is an excellent way to look at self-control and willpower and why some people find a great deal of self-control in the early stages of looking to change their lifestyle, like emotional eating, only to find it gets harder and harder. Again I think this comes back to how many hurdles, challenges and difficult emotions you face in daily life that can deplete self-control, allowing emotional eating to then kick in.

Keep firmly in mind that despite self-control being a theme in your life, perhaps from childhood, you might lack adequate amounts of it when it comes to issues with your weight. Because all the willpower and self-control in the world may not be enough if something's hurt you, damaged you or left you feeling low, and you discover at least temporary relief in emotional eating.

Can you see a pattern emerging?

Perhaps you're now seeing a pattern emerge with these three key aspects of personality—confidence versus lack of confidence, extrovert versus introvert, and now impulsive versus controlled. The pattern that emerges is this: if you fall at the more extreme end of these scales, your reaction is likely to be the same when you're stressed, unhappy or angry. There are of course different reasons and causes but you emotionally eat. It's amazing how different our personalities can be and yet how similar the reactions are to the same uncomfortable emotions.

Increasingly it's recognised that people who are addicted to one thing like drugs, alcohol or sex, frequently have cross addictions with other things, for example emotional eating. It's terribly important if you think you have an addiction/s to get the appropriate help immediately before worrying about your potential emotional eating.

What have you taken from this chapter on personality and emotional eating? Take a moment to look at the headlines above to remind you of some important things that relate to you. I highly recommend putting pen to paper here in this space to make a few notes to yourself.

CHAPTER 3

Your Emotional Life and Emotional Eating

If your emotions are consuming you then you may be consuming comfort food

Let's look more closely at your emotional life. The emotions you experience on a daily basis, plus any major emotional experiences in your past, play a big part in what for some can be a lifelong battle with food. For others, their emotional experiences mean that emotional eating is occasional, or goes through phases, when their emotions are particularly turbulent.

There are many key emotional states that can propel you into emotional eating. These include emotions like anger, jealousy, envy, guilt, hurt and bitterness, as well as more subtle feelings of shame, embarrassment, powerlessness or helplessness.

All of these emotions affect you to varying degrees depending on the situation. They can fuel your emotional eating.

BRIEF VERSUS LONG-STANDING EMOTIONAL STATES

The more obvious emotions like anger, jealousy and hurt can well up suddenly and if managed successfully might dissolve almost as suddenly. However, there's always a risk you still head for comfort food, sometimes immediately, before you've had a chance to turn these feelings around.

You can also harbour long-standing anger and hurt as well as a long-standing sense of betrayal or jealousy. When these emotional states hang around it's like a dark cloud that hovers over your life. One friend of mine, Rebecca, 47, had been an emotional eater for as long as she could remember. She had anger about her father abandoning her mother, her sister and her when she was six. Her anger was mixed with shame that somehow she wasn't a good enough daughter for him to care about her wellbeing. Thankfully Rebecca sought counselling that helped her face, understand and manage her nearly lifelong anger. One year on, her emotional eating is almost zero.

Emotions like shame and embarrassment also have a lot to answer for when it comes to emotional eating. Because these are difficult emotions that make people feel so bad about themselves that they often result in secret snacking. But the secret snacking itself leads to these feelings too and one study found that a full third of women snack in secret. And they report feeling ashamed and embarrassed about it.

You can imagine how the complex processes in the 'triangle of emotional eating' I mentioned in the last chapter kick in here.

TRIGGERS, LONG-STANDING EMOTIONAL STATES AND THEIR INTERACTION

I've already mentioned emotional triggers, for instance in Linda's story where her manager's demands were her triggers. They sent her to secret snacking in the toilets at work. As Linda learned it's crucial to understand your emotional triggers to prevent them from having this effect on you.

It's important to understand how sometimes there are long-standing emotional states that bubble under the surface of your life, like with my friend Rebecca, and other instant, sometimes short-lived, emotional triggers.

You might not have any long-standing issues with anger, hurt, shame or other negative emotions, but you still might be an emotionally-reactive person who emotionally eats after a variety of triggers. Imagine someone I met I'll call Jason. Jason's 35, had a stable upbringing and was happily married. However, Jason was one of these passionate people who reacted quite strongly to life's events. If someone at work put him down, he'd go for a big helping of comfort food at lunch. Even if he argued about politics with his older brother he'd get worked up and out would come an extra bag of chips.

Jason worked hard at understanding his reactive emotional type and learned to face the various triggers that set him off. He used some of the coping strategies I've already mentioned like taking time out and pausing before reacting, plus doing something more positive with his emotional state like calling his wife to calm down and take his mind off the upsets of life,.

A quick EED check: Are you emotionally reactive? Do your emotions bubble up quickly or take over momentarily? Would you say you're a passionate person; do you feel things quite strongly? You may well be like Jason and although have what feels like a good life, this may lead to emotional eating.

There can obviously be an interaction between any long-standing, difficult emotional state you may be experiencing and emotional triggers. Your awareness of your long-term emotional states and the triggers that may stir up these emotions is crucial to combating your emotional eating.

IDENTIFYING THE DIFFERENT EMOTIONS YOU FEEL

With different difficult emotions potentially whirling within you at any time, it's critical that you start identifying the various issues they spring from. You might be angry at your partner for being neglectful, feel humiliated by your boss who told you off in front of colleagues or feel hurt that your mother speaks to your brother more often. Each of these needs tackling because they each come from different challenges.

When you're full of conflicting emotions, it's always helpful to 'think-in-ink'—write down how you're feeling about each troubling issue. Then put them in order of importance to tackle. Once they're on paper, structured for you to challenge one at a time, you can start getting practical about them. Being practical and setting goals to sort these things out has phenomenal power for taking the sting out of your emotions.

Take one issue that troubles you now and causes the emotional pain that leads to comfort eating and write out a few steps to reach your goal to tackle this:

*   The issue: (e.g., your partner is hurtful)
*   The emotion/s it causes you: (e.g., hurt, humiliation)
*   Your goal: (e.g., getting them to understand this)

Step 1:_____

_____

Step 2:_____

_____

Step 3:_____

_____

Step 4:_____

_____

Step 5:_____

_____

Many people report that simply writing down challenging issues that cause painful emotions, and thinking through possible steps to solutions, fires them up to resist emotionally eating that day.

ONE DAY AT A TIME

This may be one of the most important points I make in the EED—so please remember this. Write it down, put it on your dressing table, at your desk, on your fridge door, on the cupboard doors or anywhere else that's prominent for you.

All of us, no matter what we're tackling, must tackle it one day at a time. This is an important rule of any twelve-step programme where people are managing addictions. Think of this rule for living well and changing your life and emotional eating as involving three elements:

The past: you can't change what's happened in days already past. Yes, you can celebrate joyous memories and, yes, you can make amends or learn from things you've done wrong in the past and you can ensure that what others have done to you in the past doesn't happen again. But you cannot relive any single day from the past.

The present: the only thing we have is today. We have control over how we respond to what happens today and we can try our best to make it the best day possible. Today is the day you can do all in your power not to emotionally eat but instead to respond to challenging situations and emotions to the best of your abilities. Today you can make a difference to yourself, your life and others you care about!

The future: none of us knows what tomorrow holds for us. It's fantastic and a good idea to make plans for the future but always with an open and flexible mind. You can't control the future, so keep focused on the emotional eating you're trying to change today.

THE DOUBLE WHAMMY: DIFFICULT EMOTIONS PLUS EMOTIONAL EATING

We all must come to terms with, manage, control and not be controlled by unhappy, difficult, challenging emotions. As an emotional eater there's the double whammy of difficult emotions springing from issues and challenges in your life, plus those unhappy emotions of yours about emotional eating—this is the complicated triangle that we mustn't lose sight of coping with.

This is why I stress the importance of unpicking this whirlwind of emotions one at a time. It helps you recognise perhaps primary negative feelings about, for example, your work, your relationships or your friendships. Then on top of these the unhappy, negative feelings arising directly from emotional eating—very often the guilt, shame, helplessness and hopelessness that I've mentioned.

Our emotional relationship with food isn't always straightforward. It's not necessarily as simple as, 'I'm stressed so I want to eat some cake now'. If it was that straightforward it might be easier to stop yourself when you're heading for the biscuit tin.

We must not underestimate the power of eating to supposedly soothe so many different emotions. I believe the misconnection between mind and mouth occurs quite easily in our modern stressful lifestyles with the availability of many addictive, supposedly 'comforting' foods. For our ancient ancestors, this mind–mouth link was completely about survival.

Obviously, we need food to live and it's wonderful to socialise over meals. But what I've noticed in talking to many people about their relationship with food is, at a very basic level, those who feel under 'threat' (like the modern threats found in the workplace or in complicated family relationships) feel compelled to emotionally eat. Basic survival becomes linked with emotional survival for emotional eaters. Unfortunately, this is an unhappy and unhealthy way of surviving.

FOOD AND FEELINGS CHECKLIST

There will be more on our relationship with food in a moment. But first, identifying your feelings about food related to emotional eating is important. We touched on this already in various ways but here's a quick checklist to give you a guide. Discover a little more about *you* now!

There's no point in dishonesty—choose your real reaction to each statement. You're only cheating yourself if you don't start to 'own' your emotional eating.

1. If I feel upset I definitely eat more   YES / NO

2. I frequently regret something I've eaten in the heat of the moment   YES / NO

3. I often feel hurt by others but don't say anything—instead I snack   YES / NO

4. When I'm upset I feel I have little control over my emotions   YES / NO

5. It's an automatic habit to think of eating/snacking if something bad happens   YES / NO

6. When stressed, I'm focused on what my next meal is going to be   YES / NO

7. I feel better at least temporarily when I eat when I'm upset   YES / NO

8. I have a favourite snack food to eat when I'm upset   YES / NO

9. I envy, even dislike, those who have an effortless relationship with food   YES / NO

10. Others (e.g., ex-partners) have made me feel bad about my eating habits   YES / NO

11. When I think about my eating habits I actually want to go snack more   **YES / NO**

12. I feel guilty, hopeless, helpless or angry with myself when I emotionally eat   **YES / NO**

13. If I have something on my mind, but can't talk about it, I eat more   **YES / NO**

14. I dislike/hate myself for the snacking and excessive eating I do   **YES / NO**

15. I sometimes blame others when they've upset me for the snacking I do   **YES / NO**

There's no way of softening the truth, but selecting even one yes-answer suggests you're prone to, if not already, emotional eating. The more yes-answers, the more intense and frequent your emotional eating may be. The point of this checklist is to focus you on the power of the relationship between your feelings and food intake.

Ideally, we're now aiming for you being in control of your emotions, not letting them run away with you and not heading down an unhappy path of snacking for the wrong reasons.

Some solutions to try from today:

Your food-friendly motto: Devise a saying that's a 'rally cry' for you—anything that works for you as your daily affirmation. For instance try, 'I can get on top of emotional eating when I tackle the things that upset me'. Or, 'One day at a time. When I face my emotions head-on I'll do better with emotional eating'.

Challenge your need: Challenge yourself about your present thinking—deep down are you actually stronger than you give yourself credit for? So many emotional eaters I've met over the years actually have powerful levels of inner strength but convince themselves that they don't. When you're challenged by difficult emotions, challenge your reaction. Do they have to affect you so deeply? Can you actually handle them? Have you been underestimating your inner strength?

'Take five' before food: Here's that pause again—compose yourself before you eat any snack or meal. If you've rushed for something sweet, fattening and essentially what seems comforting, try calming down before you start eating. With your daily affirmation, your self-challenging and your newfound understanding of emotional eating, you might be able to resist emotional eating at that moment.

Picture the happier you: Keep a picture of you smiling and happy as your laptop wallpaper or homepage. Also keep it handy on your phone to look at and remind yourself you're heading for happier times. Research shows it's helpful to have pictures of ourselves from the good times handy to bring back happy memories. They remind us that life isn't always sad, bad or mad.

Keep your hands busy: This is one of those behavioural traits that an emotional eater often develops—the need to feel something between their fingertips. Worry beads can fill that gap or you can take up something like knitting, as so many celebrities do.

Focus on the positive: Start each day focusing on what's important to you. Keep that squarely in mind so that the small stuff (or the big stuff) doesn't bring you down. You might make your daily positive-focus on the blessings in your life, something good that no one can take away from you.

Accept the truth: Here is a truth about your emotional eating that you must accept, and this acceptance will make you stronger: As I said earlier in this chapter you must 'own' your emotional eating and not hide from it. Hold firmly in mind the fact that only when you start to feel more positively about yourself and you can accept your emotional eating has been a symptom of unhappiness, stress or another negative emotion, will things start to change for you— ultimately, your weight and wellbeing.

Don't try too hard: Throwing yourself 100 per cent into something new like the EED may backfire. As mentioned, research shows you can get diet-fatigue where you burn out your ability to stick to it. Don't feel you have to give 100 per cent at all times to the EED or any other life-changing plan. It's important to accept that you can only give so much, and small changes over time are far better than throwing yourself into something only to find you can't sustain that enthusiasm.

YOUR PARENTS' RELATIONSHIP WITH FOOD

How much can you remember about your parents' attitudes toward food? Because this reveals how you formed your relationship with food. For instance, when you fell over and hurt yourself did your mother rush to you with some sweets to cheer you up? Or did your mother or father arrive home from a hard day at work and immediately grab a big bag of crisps to munch?

What messages did you get as a young child when it came to eating—that food was an 'emotional-pill' and there to soothe you, offer comfort, even replace affection if your parents were busy and couldn't stop to discuss why you were upset? 'Take five' just to think about your first impressions about how your parents might have used food for emotional reasons.

Even in the good and happy times did your parents use food— and feeding you—as a reward for good behaviour? Was it always a slap-up meal with extra dessert when someone did something well? Shared family meals are fantastic and I absolutely believe in families eating together as often as possible. However, some families turn all celebrations into great feasts where people stuff and gorge themselves well beyond a healthy point. Yes, this emotional eating comes from a happy place but isn't good for your long-term health.

It's absolutely fine to do this occasionally, and don't we all do it on holidays like Christmas? But when a family always uses an excess of food to celebrate anything and everything and positively encourages people to have that second or third helping of dessert to celebrate something, it can be a very slippery slope to emotional eating.

Food as punishment

Some families also use food as a punishment if you've been 'naughty'. When you misbehaved perhaps you were given only a small portion of dinner or no dinner at all? Maybe you weren't allowed dessert while the rest of the family tucked into a delicious one. Or perhaps you were forced to have extra helpings of your least favourite food (typically green vegetables for many young children) and expected to eat every last bit. Such treatment can affect your way of coping with life's difficulties and potentially lead to issues such as secret snacking. And when food is used as punishment, it can lead to people craving what they don't have as in Robert's case below.

Robert's emotional eating experience

Robert, 39, a history teacher, confessed to having been a secret snacker for years. His earliest memories gave him a sense that he was happy-go-lucky as a young child. But he recalled how from mid-childhood onwards, once he had a younger brother and sister, food was always used as a punishment or a reward by his mother, now busy with three children and working part time.

When Robert was 'good' he was given as much dessert as he could wolf down. When Robert was 'bad' he was sent to bed without dinner with the door closed on his bedroom—it's a very lonely place being shut behind the door for a young child.

Robert started hoarding his favourite foods because more often than not he was punished for his 'bad' behaviour. Robert admitted he was quite clumsy and it was only in his early thirties he realised he was dyspraxic and less physically coordinated than others.

His parents used to accuse him of things such as knocking things over or being malicious by bumping into his younger sister or brother. You can imagine how bewildering this was to a young child who had no intention of harming his younger siblings or knocking over his mother's favourite vase.

His secret snacking meant he hadn't been a healthy weight for many years. It also meant he had developed a secretive side. Robert never told his wife how he was feeling about various things—he just got on with life. He never told her anything bad or negative from work and certainly didn't tell her about his secret snack stash. It was only when Robert's wife discovered his stash of chocolates and sweets that Robert opened up about his emotional eating.

Despite his emotional eating now in the open, Robert feared, as he'd always been like this, that he couldn't change the compulsion to run for his stash when things got a little tough.

Emotional energiser solution: Robert could finally accept his emotional eating had led to much unhappiness. He realised he needed to change, and as a result how much better his relationship with his wife would be, as well as his relationship with food.

Trigger identification: After only a couple days of keeping his food diary, Robert could see quite clearly how often he dipped into his hoard of snacks when he had an issue with a pupil or if he thought about the evening's workload of marking.

Trigger specifics: What was it about a pupil talking out of turn or being loud that bothered Robert so much? A detailed discussion revealed it reminded him of his own parent–child relationship. He realised how much his parents must have felt stressed with his clumsiness and 'bad behaviour'. This jumble of thoughts about the past, stimulated by the children he taught, caused him anxiety and his solution was snacking.

In addition to this, his evening workload cut into family time, and as he'd been hiding part of his genuine self from his family this caused him guilt—again leading to emotional eating.

Trigger tips: The starting point for Robert was to identify his urges to be secretive. He agreed on a plan with his wife where each evening she would ask about his day and he was to answer honestly, including any stresses from work.

* Instead of his secret stash Robert now keeps a snack box in the kitchen with a set number of snacks that count as treats—one per day after work. Please note, some people find it works to allow themselves one treat a day and others have to cut out treats entirely as having one means they just feel they have to have another. You have the power inside you to discover what works for you as an individual.
* Robert discussed with the head teacher better behavioural management techniques that he could employ with his pupils. The head teacher was surprised when Robert wanted this discussion because, of course, Robert had been secretive about his classroom struggles.
* Each day he entered the classroom with a newfound belief that whatever his pupils tried to get away with was no reflection on some of the unhappy issues from his past. Today was today and the past had passed.
* He created a daily self-affirmation about the here and now whenever unhappy childhood memories came to mind.

Overall, Robert made enormous strides forward with his emotional eating. He faced his impulses head-on and it paid off as he slowly but steadily lost his excess weight.

Robert's story is a classic example of how your past, and secrecy, can affect your present-day emotional eating. Sharing your difficulties with those who count at home or at work can make an enormous difference. This was an important step forward for Robert, as it is for all of us.

THE FOOD OF LOVE

When you're hungry for love and support, it may become confused with being hungry for food if you can't find a way of managing the emotional need.

I find a very big aspect of emotional eating is how it links in with love. Just think of my personal experience with emotional eating when I was so worried about the wellbeing of my baby-to-be during my second pregnancy and was not receiving the love and support I needed.

The connection between food and love is strong. When we meet someone, our first and subsequent dates often involve sharing meals. And when we're in love we frequently use food in a playful way: we feed each other, we give each other gifts of food, we get rude with food in the bedroom, and we continue to have candlelit meals. When love breaks our heart, this behaviour can continue but for the opposite reason—in a dysfunctional way it reminds you of what you shared when you were in love. It also temporarily soothes us when actually we need to turn to family or friends for soothing. We also need to find strength in our ability to self-soothe.

Many of you will know how a powerful triangle of emotional eating kicks in with a broken heart. Your heart's broken, you eat to relieve it, then punish yourself with more emotional pain because you gave in to snacking—and so each corner of the triangle is fulfilled repeatedly.

well as happiness. In fact, when you've overcome difficult and challenging situations and feelings, you become the best person you can be—someone with empathy, someone with fight and spirit and someone who will make better choices.

Please remember the most important lesson of this chapter is that if things are eating away at your heart and soul then you're likely to emotionally eat. It's time to look at how you can pinpoint what leads to emotional eating with your food and feelings diary.

CHAPTER 4

Keeping Your Food and Feelings Diary

Get to know your feelings, get to know your emotional eating

You are now going to become a type of 'journalist' of your emotional eating. You'll be asking the what, when, where, how and why of your emotional eating habits.

You are probably wondering why I didn't put this in the first chapter. It might seem logical that you would fill out your food and feelings diary as an important first step to discovering more about your emotional eating. However, from my experience it's important to first learn something about your food and feelings, as you have from the last few chapters, because this means you're better prepared to fill in your food diary and ultimately you'll gain more benefit.

Another thing you might be thinking is, 'Help! This is going to be too much work.' Trust me, it's not. It's really nothing compared to how much real, hard work it is when you resist facing up to the emotional demands of your life; or compared to how draining it is to carry around excess weight; or compared to trying to contain your anxieties about your weight. Those things take a much greater emotional and physical toll on you.

WHAT YOUR DIARY SHOULD REVEAL

The crucial part about your food and feelings diary is learning about your 'hot spots'. Those emotional triggers that set off a desire for emotional eating. If someone asks you what causes you stress, anger or hurt., off the top of your head, you could undoubtedly list some things. But what I almost always find is when someone starts recording what sets them down the path of emotional eating, or when they look back at their diary at the end of a week or two, there are always revelations. It is these revelations that keep you on your toes for the various situations, issues or people (yes those people who push our buttons) you must pay attention to. Otherwise those urges to emotionally eat sneak under the wire of your consciousness. Or they slip over the wire of your consciousness and you're absolutely aware of them, but feel unable at the time to stop them.

I want you to look at these things in black and white so you can't be in denial about what upsets you, or avoid deciding how you will tackle your triggers.

WHAT'S YOUR POISON?

By keeping your diary you'll soon see the food types you head for—your personal 'poison', as the saying goes—and you might find this knowledge helpful for combating those cravings. It's important to look for a link between your particular poison and whether it's related to any particular mood state? For instance, are you a sweet-treat freak when stressed or a savoury-craver when unhappy? Or maybe your mood dictates the comfort food of choice?

Although the author of one book on cravings suggests that specific cravings have specific meanings behind them, I tend to take a more flexible approach. However, it's interesting to see that Dr Doreen Virtue suggests that craving creamy foods is related to insecurity and anxiety, as the creaminess may well be seen as relaxing and comforting. Also, she suggests that a craving for crunchy things like popcorn or crisps suggests you're overstressed. Evidently the crunching action helps release the stress, but it's far better to have crunchy snacks like carrots, celery and nuts than buttery popcorn or deep-fried crisps. Such thinking is important in that it supports the whole idea of emotional eating and how cravings might be driven by different emotions.

I strongly believe that you as an individual may well have your own pattern of cravings. This dictates which particular type of food you'll choose at that moment when emotionally eating.

COMPLETING YOUR FOOD AND FEELINGS DIARY

Let's get started! First some notes on keeping your diary:

* Organise either an online diary on your laptop, mobile or tablet, or a paper notepad diary.
* Ideally when you're starting out you should keep a food and feelings diary for two weeks, but one week will do if there's any chance you will find two weeks too much.
* Whether online or in notepad-form, your diary must be with you at all times.
* Each time you eat (including all main meals and of course all snacking) make your entry and the time of day for each.
* Your entries don't have to be detailed as long as you include the key information.
* You should do a trial run to see how much space you need. In a notepad diary you might find you need one, two or more pages per day.
* Finally, record the following five things: the trigger, your thought/s, prevention behaviour, negative feelings, and positive feelings. These are defined below.

Trigger: What started you thinking about food? Was it something that happened to you at work, a row with your partner or something else? Is this a regular emotional trigger? Was it a new emotional trigger?

Thoughts: What was going through your mind as you snacked or ate a meal? For example, were you thinking what relief you were getting at that moment from eating, or worrying about what you were doing?

Prevention: Did you try to make any attempt not to have a snack or unnecessary meal? If so, what did you do? Did it work or did it fail?

Negative feelings: If you couldn't stop yourself from eating, how did you feel after your snack or unnecessary meal? For example, did you feel angry with yourself, disgusted, unhappy, upset, numb?

Positive feelings: If you did stop yourself from eating, how did you feel about that? Did you feel proud, happy, relieved, still anxious?

Here's a sample entry from someone I met through work who I'll call Sarah. She's in her twenties and works in PR. Sarah's mother is a classic 'feeder' who always fed her family in the hard times or in the good times alike. Her mother's solution for any emotional time, event or issue was to bake a big batch of biscuits or a cake.

Sarah kept a food and feelings diary and found repeated entries like the following:

Thursday, 3 p.m.:

Trigger: A client wasn't happy with my PR campaign suggestion.

Thoughts: I felt stupid and that the client would never take me seriously again.

Prevention: I didn't take any prevention. I simply popped out to the café next to work and bought a big piece of carrot cake.

Negative feelings: I feel guilty and useless having eaten the piece of cake. I feel I have no control. I feel no one will take me seriously.

Positive feelings: I have no positive feelings this afternoon.

This demonstrates a good, succinct diary entry, but you can make yours far more detailed. Sarah was shocked at how much she was turning to food during the fortnight she kept this diary. It was a real wake-up call for her to get on top of negative emotions.

After keeping your diary for at least a week, it's time to analyse it. Here's what to look for:

*   What are your main triggers, the things that usually cause emotional eating?
*   What are your secondary or more unusual triggers?
*   What is your main feeling after giving in to emotional eating?
*   If you did stop yourself from emotional eating, how did you manage that?
*   What made that situation different and what can you learn from this alternative, positive behaviour to take into other trigger situations

Make a note here of what's worked for you, even if it only worked on one occasion.

_____
_____
_____
_____
_____
_____
_____
_____
_____
_____
_____
_____
_____
_____
_____
_____
_____
_____
_____
_____

Once you've kept your diary, take a little time to generate other potential solutions that spring to mind. For instance, when you headed for that unnecessary snack after your boss asked you to do extra work, could you have picked up the phone to a friend instead and had a five-minute break and a friendly chat? This, or one of many other things like a brisk five-minute walk, could have helped you compose your tricky emotions.

Identifying the 'new you':

If you were asked to define yourself right now you'd probably include a fair few negatives, especially if asked to describe yourself and your relationship with food. Now is the time to start defining the new you. Tell yourself you have the power within you to handle your emotions without emotional eating that from now on you will not be defined as an emotional eater but as someone who's changing the way they handle their emotions. Identify appropriate responses to tricky, difficult and downright damaging emotions: By now you will be identifying your negative responses to emotions—those responses include your emotional eating. Can you think of a recent example where you had an appropriate response to an issue or otherwise negative situation? What happened that helped you to handle it? Focus on the fact that you can identify some appropriate responses you've made.

Accept that your emotions are normal and okay to have:

It's crucial that you now start to accept that you are entitled to difficult, 'stressy', tricky, big and small emotions. There is nothing wrong with your emotions! You are absolutely justified having these—they are part of our makeup—and what you need to do is respond to them in positive and healthy ways.

Appropriate responses to difficult emotions:
*   Reassure yourself that it's okay to feel that way. It's not the end of the world and the feeling will pass.
*   Make a plan of how to tackle whatever has created a difficult

emotion within you. What can you do about the situation? What do you expect anyone else involved to do about it?

* You have your expectations in mind for your part in the situation, and your expectations for someone else's part in the situation, now how can you move this forward? Do you need to discuss this with them? Do you need to make suggestions to them?

* If you need to talk to another person involved, to tackle them or challenge them, use the '3Ps':
  PLAN what needs to be done,
  PRACTISE what you need to say and
  PUT it into action.

* Moving on from your action, tell yourself that you have done your best, accept what you might have done differently, learn from this event and set your boundaries in future if something similar arises.

REFLECTION ON YOUR FOOD AND FEELINGS DIARY

A little reflection on what you may have discovered in your diary—and hopefully you'll discover a number of interesting, insightful things—will be extremely helpful. It's interesting that when you see things written down you can actually see the 'misconnection' between your mind and mouth in action. How—when you should be eating for energy and social reasons—what's going on in your mind leads to unnecessary emotional eating. Getting a visual take on this misconnection can be very powerful. Whenever possible take a moment to look at a passage in your diary. Or make an occasional 'day diary' where you just record things for a day to see what's happening in black and white at that time.

We don't take enough time to reflect on our lives, our selves and our emotions in our busy lifestyles. The whole mindfulness movement is about taking the time to be mindful of what you're doing at that moment. This is like a series of mini-reflections about what's going on and what's driving you in your behaviour, especially your eating behaviour.

You've committed to learning about your emotional eating so it's vital you commit to keeping a food and feelings diary. It's absolutely worth the effort—the payoff for most people is fantastic! Yes, some effort is involved, so look at your diary and choose a week very soon that doesn't involve any big events like, for example, moving house, that will add enormous additional stress to your usual level of stress.

Give yourself a starting date and stick to it—it matters to you and your emotional eating. Let your diary help give you clues as to what underlies the eating habits that are all about your emotions.

CHAPTER 5

Your Love–Hate Relationship with Food

The thing we love can also be the thing we come to hate

Let's explore in more depth your personal relationship with food. It will help you enormously in the changes you want to make if you start viewing this as a 'relationship'. How you relate to food and eating, the emotions that compel you to eat when it's not necessary and the emotions that spring from that are a relationship. As you're now beginning to understand (and probably already understood to some extent), this relationship can be dysfunctional and emotionally unhealthy—truly a very personal, love–hate affair. Think of this love–hate relationship with food as similar in strength to a dysfunctional emotional relationship. If you haven't been in that kind of relationship yourself, you have undoubtedly seen a friend or family member go through one.

These love–hate relationships are characterised by two partners who treat each other badly but neither of them seem willing to break free. It's a hard habit to break and the power of a dysfunctional love–hate affair should never be underestimated. The two partners stick at it for a variety of reasons. Maybe they've always known this type of romantic relationship as that's how their parents related, or perhaps they had a trauma in one relationship (or in life) that has left them with damaged self-esteem and expecting further trauma. They may have an immature personality and don't know how to cope with the inevitable ups and downs in relationships, so they battle with a partner, make up and fall out again. There are many other potential reasons.

Is any of the above reminding you of what I've discussed in previous chapters, like your parents' influence on your personality or how trauma or an unhappy experience might influence how you feel about yourself? There are parallels between food and staying in an unhappy relationship. We love it and the immediate comfort it offers, and we end up hating it because we hate the negative emotions and weight gain associated with it. Plus deep down we know we need to handle life's ups and downs differently and not emotionally eat.

I mentioned the 'food of love' in chapter 3, and how the love you might crave, but don't receive, can leave you emotionally eating. Not receiving love is, sadly, an excellent example of how we end up in a love–hate relationship with food. Just as we crave love—a natural human emotion—we may look for it in the wrong people or in the wrong ways, in what might be called a dysfunctional or even obsessive love. This type of relationship can be self-punishing. It is possible to think you love someone, but there can be a lot of animosity, negative and even hateful feelings between you. These have a parallel to the love–hate feelings we can feel after emotionally eating.

Take a moment to reflect on how you might be in a love–hate relationship with food. Is the way you emotionally eat a form of self-punishment? Is the calm you feel if you know there's a big comforting snack waiting for you in your desk, for example, after you finish a challenging meeting, a little obsessive?

Make a note here of what the phrase 'having a love–hate relationship with food' brings to mind for you:

_____

_____

_____

_____

_____

_____

_____

Samantha's emotional eating experience

Samantha is one of the many people I interviewed over the last four or five years with the intention of one day writing the EDD. Samantha is in her fifties. She is twice divorced and works in the legal profession. She noticed her emotional eating had increased over the years. To look at Samantha, you wouldn't know she was anything but super confident and in control of every aspect of her life. That's how she portrays herself to the world—on top of her game in a competitive area of law and beautifully turned out, even down to her vibrant matching pink lipstick and nail polish.

Samantha had always been aware of fitness and eating well, but after her first divorce at age 35 she found herself eating cakes and chocolate for the first time. She was extremely hard on herself about this—truly self-punishing. Every time Samantha indulged in sweet things to excess she felt awful and threw herself into even longer hours at work. She hated the fact she had put on six kilograms on top of what she considered her normal and healthy weight.

When Samantha remarried, a marriage she thought would be 'forever', she gained control of the emotional eating for a time. But as that marriage fell apart it came back with a vengeance. Again she found her emotional eating increasing and again she battered herself with even longer hours at work, punishing gym routines and lots of Botox and other cosmetic enhancements.

Samantha wasn't someone who found balance in her life. Instead she threw herself 100 per cent into everything. When she 'happened upon' emotional eating it was essentially the same—she emotionally ate with a vengeance.

Samantha felt such anger at herself and questioned why, when she was so in control of her work, her social life with her girlfriends, physical fitness, personal grooming and other aspects of her life, she couldn't seem to control her emotional eating. Where was the emotional pain driving this behaviour really coming from? Partly it was from the pain of her failed relationships and partly from her perfectionist nature.

Emotional energiser solution: Samantha described to me how after seeing a relationship counsellor to get more insight into her failed marriages she became much more aware of how hard she was on herself and also how difficult she found it to face painful events.

This was a real wake-up call for her and led her to accept that facing these things would help her face up to her emotional eating. Despite the apparent successes of her life making it seem that everything was in control, she wasn't emotionally in control.

Samantha described how she had embraced with gusto—as she did with everything else in her life—the fact that she was going to have to start facing painful emotions the way she faced any problem at work: head on.

Trigger identification: In our interview Samantha described how once her counselling sessions had finished she took forward what she had learnt about her perfectionism and relationships. She identified what I'd describe as her triggers. The main two triggers for her emotional eating were: (1) Reminders of her two divorces; and (2) When she felt fearful about meeting someone to spend the rest of her life with.

Trigger specifics: In Samantha's case these reminders simply made her feel like a failure. And Samantha did not handle failure well before she had counselling.

Trigger tips: I was delighted to hear that Samantha had established her own self-challenging when feelings of failure had sent her to emotionally eat. She described how she had become so much better at knowing when a negative emotion was gripping her, how to talk herself down from feeling angry with herself and how to let it go.

Samantha now has emotional eating pretty much under control. She's back at a healthy and energetic weight and was very honest in saying that only occasionally does her perfectionist streak get the better of her and that's when she's at risk of having, for example, a second helping of dessert that she doesn't need.

PERFECTIONISM AND EMOTIONAL EATING

Thinking of Samantha's experience brings to mind how we view perfectionists as go-getters and high achievers. This is often the case, and they are often those people who appear to excel at everything they turn their hand to. I think it's increasingly accepted, though, that perfectionists often struggle with deep insecurities that drive them to try to be perfect.

When we think about what a so-called 'emotional eater' might be like, some people might assume just the opposite. They assume they have quite negative traits: for instance that they're greedy, lazy or don't care about letting themselves go. These are terrible generalisations that simply aren't true. And I've found in my work, in interviewing people for this book and with my own friends that frequently those who emotionally eat are 'perfectionists of their emotions'. By this I mean that they are people who don't want to see themselves as having negative emotions, or who don't feel they should have negative emotions when other people are worse off than they are. They are very goodhearted people who simply care too much about presenting a positive face to the world, and in private they don't let themselves face difficult emotions.

This is anecdotal, but I'm speaking about the experiences and attitudes of so many people who've confided in me. I mentioned this feeling of having to be perfect at the end of chapter 3 and now I want you to think of it in broad terms and how it might relate to your emotional eating. Are you an emotional perfectionist who finds it hard to accept that difficult, stressful, bad or hurtful things happen to you? Does this lead you to being too hard on yourself in life, with your outlet being emotional eating?

Perfectionism, weight and size

Perfectionism also, and rather dangerously, can lead into unrealistic expectations for your weight. I prefaced the EDD with the warning that if you had an eating disorder you needed to get appropriate help, and here we're potentially 'skirting the rim' of this territory. You need to be honest with yourself about whether you are basically fit and well but emotionally beat yourself up for not fitting into, for example, your pre-pregnancy jeans? It's easy to buy into the pressure to be perfect and stop appreciating *you* for the person you are.

It's crucial that if you recognise yourself as a perfectionist who strives to have the perfect physique and stay on the thin side that you keep aware of this. And if in the past you've ever restricted food intake because you want to be 'perfect', it's crucial that you treat yourself, your eating habits and your emotions with the greatest care. As I've written the EED for the many people who simply need to get on top of emotional eating so they can stay a happy healthy weight and not put on excess weight, I'm not going to dwell on the more serious side of perfectionism.

Forgive yourself

Perfectionists and emotional eaters, and those who combine both of these traits, also find it hard to forgive themselves when they've made a mistake, done something wrong or maybe fallen below their very high standards. Forgiving yourself is absolutely crucial for your wellbeing and moving on.

YOUR FOOD-RELATED HABITS

Almost everything we do is part of a series of habits. Think about your morning routine. I bet you do the same thing each and every morning: from your dressing routine, bathroom routine, breakfast routine, getting-out-the-door routine, it's the same. We streamline our lives with habits that become our routines. This isn't necessarily a bad thing, as chains of behaviour like your morning habits, or cleaning-your-home habits, tend to speed things up. However, as an emotional eater, it's the bad food habits you develop that need to be identified and broken. Once you manage this, you start to establish good food habits.

Classic bad food habits of emotional eaters include the chain of behaviour from something that has upset you to putting food in your mouth. For instance, an acquaintance, Marianne, a 45-year-old marketing director, described the following chain of behaviours:

A colleague criticises her work (evidently this colleague does this fairly frequently):

* Inside Marianne feels extremely hurt, thinking, 'Why me? What have I done? Why don't they like me?"
* Marianne opens the stash drawer in her desk.
* She fingers various treats she keeps in there.
* She then takes the third treat in the drawer—in her own mind leaving it to 'fate' how big or small this snack is.
* Marianne walks to the coffee area and eats the snack.
* Marianne is immediately guilt-ridden and unhappy that she has emotionally eaten.

Evidently, this chain of behaviour—Marianne's habitual response to emotional hurt—happens exactly this way every time. There are other chains of behaviour in Marianne's day that leads to emotional eating but I hope that gives you an idea of why you need to be mindful of such chains of behaviour. Identifying little rituals and habits that lead to emotional eating will help you break them.

Identify one chain of behaviour that's an emotional eating habit of yours. You might need more or fewer steps:

Behaviour 1._____

Behaviour 2._____

Behaviour 3._____

Behaviour 4._____

Behaviour 5._____

The Autopilot of Emotional Eating

Your habits of emotional eating may or may not surprise you. They'll surprise you if you don't realise how easily you can go on autopilot with emotional eating. As I've mentioned, so many of our habits are automatic and this is no different.

When you start to identify your own autopilot it becomes a matter of mind over mouth. Your active awareness means you can stop the automatic habit. 'Active' is the key word: you have to actively be aware of your behaviour while you're retraining yourself to cope with emotions and stopping the destructive triangle of emotional eating.

Emotional Eater Energiser: When that little devil on your shoulder starts giving you a hard time, chattering about a mistake you've just made, face it down. Always look at how you can rectify a situation, what you can learn from it and then allow yourself to move on. Forgiveness will help you prevent emotional eating—something you're much more likely to do when you're telling yourself you're an 'awful' or 'silly' person.

Become actively aware

To become actively aware means that you start living in the moment rather than fast-forwarding to what you're doing tomorrow, next week or even next year. You also don't throw back to the past. Becoming actively aware is the one-day-at-a-time way of living I stressed in chapter 3.

Becoming actively aware of any automatic side to your habitual behaviour is necessary for you to be able to take control of it. This is another reason why your food and feelings diary is a must-do, because when you look back at it you may realise how much you go on autopilot with your emotional eating.

YOUR ESSENTIAL EMOTIONAL EATER PROFILE

A bit more understanding of your essential emotional-eater profile can help switch off this automatic behaviour. The following mini-questionnaire might illuminate a deeper understanding of your personal love–hate affair with food. Answer honestly and see which profile best matches your answers:

1. When are you most likely to emotionally eat?
A. When I'm angry with someone or myself.
B. When I'm feeling stressed and that I can't cope.
C. When I'm doubting myself and feeling I'm not 'good enough'.
D. When something reminds me of a painful experience/s I've had.

2. If you think someone's neglecting you, 'slighting' you or basically undermining you, what's your most likely reaction?
A. I feel very angry inside.
B. Wondering why they're behaving that way makes me stressed.
C. It makes it hard for me to feel good about anything the rest of the day.
D. It makes me feel how I always feel—that life will always be tough for me.

3. If you could change just one thing about your emotions, which of the following would you choose?
A. I'd change my feelings of anger.
B. I'd change my stress levels and how I handle stress .
C. I'd get rid of my feelings of insecurity.
D. I'd stop feeling so much pain from the past.

4. If you have to face someone about an issue, what's your biggest fear?

A. That I'll erupt and won't be able to control my temper.

B. That no matter what, I'll just keep worrying about it.

C. That I'll back down because I'm no good at arguing.

D. That it's going to be too painful and bring up all sorts of hurtful feelings.

5. What's most likely going through your mind as you emotionally eat?

A. How angry I am at a person or situation and/or how angry I am at myself.

B. How unbearable the stress is and how I want it to change.

C. How I wish I could lean on someone at that moment.

D. How much I don't care at that moment about hurting myself or gaining weight with excess food.

Please count up how many As, Bs, Cs and Ds you circled and make a note here:

As:_____

Bs:_____

Cs:_____

Ds:_____

Please note that even if you don't have mainly A answers it is essential you read the advice below, as anger features in so many different aspects of emotional eating. It's a big part of your love–hate affair with food. You can then move on to check the advice for your most frequent answers, but also look at the other advice for mainly Bs, Cs and Ds.

Mainly As: Angry eater

This would suggest that feeling angry towards others or situations, or turned in towards yourself, is the key trigger you need to become more aware of. Those who harbour angry emotions and don't usually let it out, or eventually let it out in angry outbursts, can find emotional eating takes over because their anger becomes a constant emotional presence bubbling under the surface.

Anger is a big deal for you and your wellbeing, and quite apart from emotional eating, those who carry around a lot of anger are also more prone to heart disease. There's also a link between anger and hypertension: high blood pressure. If hypertension is left unchecked it can become a serious health condition. And that's actually something to get angry about! Again, on top of emotional eating, an undesirable side effect of chronic anger is that it can lead to higher stress levels. The stress hormone cortisol is then released into your system, and that's linked to other health problems. Let's not forget that those with anger issues also experience more tension headaches and other symptoms like a feeling of tightness in the chest and/or palpitations.

Finally, for those concerned about the aging process, another side-effect of carrying around too much anger is that you're more likely to scowl and end up with frown lines instead of happy smile 'crinkles'. So there are a whole lot of reasons why you should take on board these tips to deal with your anger:

* As I've already said in the EED, you're entitled to your feelings, and if something makes you angry, and the anger is justifiable, then you need to 'own' your anger. This anger tells you that the situation needs to be rectified. So listen to it.

* Keep a Dictaphone with you or get a voice-activated app for your phone so you can record angry thoughts when they spring up. Make a point of listening back to these at the end of each day. It's crucial you really understand your angry feelings as it makes it easier to choose an appropriate response. Putting them down on tape, so to speak, also helps get them out of your system.

* As you listen back to your angry feelings can you see a way

forward? Can you plan a goal for resolving the issue that made you angry? If so, start planning your steps to reach that goal for each issue.

*   Here's a crucial thought for people who harbour a lot of anger: challenge your negative belief system that there's always someone or something to blame for things. I've found that those with anger problems often want to point the finger or have a scapegoat for anything from the minor to the major irritations of life. Instead, start taking the 'stuff happens' attitude that there's not always someone to blame when things go wrong or you have differences of opinions with others.

*   When you feel anger welling up, remove yourself from the situation; sit-down and talk yourself out of it. To help with your impulse to emotionally eat when angry, start sorting anger into two 'zones': the zone that is important and that you need to sort out, and the zone that is not important and that you need to let go of.

*   Many of the people I meet who have anger issues have a negative—and angry—voice inside their head. I've talked about your inner voice and you need to pay particular attention if it makes you angry. Identify thinking along the lines of, 'I'll show them what's what', 'how dare they go against me' and 'who do they think they are?'. These responses to tricky situations are all about pride. You feel like you've been shown up. You feel like someone's treated you badly and you're going to 'get them'. But people who think like this usually don't resolve the problem and instead keep this angry train of thought going, then run for the comfort food because it's all too much. If you feel your inner voice is going along those bitter lines, plan to be honest with the person you're thinking these things about. Think of a solution to your difficulties and put it to them in a calm manner.

*   Certainly, many emotional eaters have difficulty with clear

communication. If they didn't have these problems then they would be communicating to others over issues. Communication and resolving issues helps prevent emotional eating. A great starting point in communication is acknowledging the positive side of whatever is to be discussed and inwardly admitting to yourself that clear communication, where you don't harbour grudges, is going to help the all-important you. It is better to get things off your chest calmly rather than stewing on them, meaning you're likely to head for that favourite snack. I provide a crucial passage on communication in the next chapter.

* One of the most important points is to identify the things that soothe and calm you. It may be particular music, in which case you should keep your MP3 player handy. Or it may be that when you feel angry, going for a brisk walk helps, or perhaps ringing a particular friend who's good at reasoning with you.

Mainly Bs: Stressed eater

Your answers reveal that feeling stressed and unable to cope with stress is probably one of the key parts of your emotional eating. I offer many strategies for dealing with stress in chapter 8 where I discuss boosting your mood to boost your ability to prevent emotional eating. However, you can begin with these two essential tips:

* From today, start saying no to extra responsibilities. By cutting your responsibilities, especially while you're working towards having a healthy way of coping with tricky emotions and a healthy relationship with food, you have a far better chance of success.

* When you feel stressed, challenge the thinking running through your mind. Is this something you really need to be stressed about? Could you dare to face it in a calm manner? Daring yourself to take a different response can open up a whole new way of responding to stress.

Mainly Cs: Insecure eater

Selecting mainly Cs suggests that your emotional eating may be mostly about feelings of insecurity and that you wish you had more support. Such feelings of insecurity can be particularly destructive, leaving a person feeling helpless when facing issues. Try these two tips to deal with your insecurity:

* Insecure people buy into the myth that everyone around them feels so much better and secure within themselves. Believe me, most of those people are 'faking it to make it'. They put on a secure front to the world that sometimes actually increases feelings of insecurity. At other times it just gets them through the day. So try a bit of 'faking it to make it' today and reassure yourself that you can cope well. Remind yourself of when you coped recently with an event or incident. Hold this firmly in mind, telling yourself that you're far from helpless.

* Be aware of the emotionally-draining 'disease to please', where people who feel insecure think they have to please others around them. They fear rejection so much that they bend over backwards to please others. This leaves you wide open to emotional eating because inside you know you're not being true to yourself. There is more on this important concept in the next chapter.

Mainly Ds: 'Emotionally wounded' eater

When it comes to emotional eating your answers suggest you've found it hard to heal past hurts, issues and painful memories. When at least a little healing hasn't taken place, it means that things that happened today bring back painful feelings from the past. Because these painful memories underlie your daily life, they're reignited in this way. Here are two tips to deal with your pain:

* It's crucial that if you've been harbouring painful memories from trauma or difficulties in your past that you get professional help. Many people I meet who are haunted

84

by painful memories feel they're not 'worth' the bother of professional help. You are! Make an appointment today to see your healthcare provider about a referral or look online for a local support group that would be relevant to you. You'll feel better knowing you've started this journey.

* For others, so much about letting go of past pain is telling yourself it's okay to do so. You have to give yourself the permission to say you can live life from today. You're allowed to say that no matter what happened in the past you've every right to enjoy a happier and more fulfilling life now.

Give yourself an emotional hug right now. Imagine comforting arms wrapping around your heart and soul. Take a moment to meditate on this calming and comforting image.

A reminder that no matter what you selected most (As, Bs, Cs or Ds), you should read all of the above passages, as many of the tips are applicable regardless of your emotional eater type.

IF YOU DON'T FIT IN YOUR JEANS, DON'T BLAME IT ON YOUR GENES

No matter where your emotional eating springs from—anger, stress, insecurity, emotional pain or a or combination of all such feelings—it's easy to start looking for something, someone or somewhere else to lay the blame. Frustration can easily lead to the blame game if you've been an emotional eater for a time and can't break the cycle. Of course, now that you're reading the EED you're ready to break the cycle.

Inwardly you get frustrated, annoyed and angry with yourself for your emotional eating, and it's a natural reaction to look outside yourself for something on which to lay the blame. Laying blame on something outside yourself is the path of denial. Doing this will mean you'll never come to terms with the truth—that being that you must be able to face, handle and manage your emotions without relating them to food.

Are you playing the blame game for emotional eating and/or excess weight? If you have a history of emotional eating then you may have other negative and potentially self-destructive behaviours preventing you from taking control of your emotions. For instance, when feeling emotionally down and perhaps disheartened about your emotional eating, it's easy to blame it on your 'fat genes'.

Today, increasing research is being done on the connection between genetics and weight gain, and yes, some research suggests about 4 per cent of people do have a so-called 'fat gene'. However, the chances are less than likely and should not be used as a scapegoat for excessive eating.

Of course, it is possible that you do have this 'fat gene' in your genetic makeup. It is still crucial that you do the best with the genetics you have been given. It is important to ensure you take responsibility for yourself and your emotional reactions instead of playing the blame game. It is interesting that one study of the so-called junk-food gene found that even those with this gene who find it harder to fight cravings still benefit from exercise. There's no excuse not to look after yourself in every way—from exercise to your emotional life.

Unfortunately for women, one study from Maastricht University revealed that we're more likely to have the flawed version of a particular gene that makes us prone to developing fatty tissue. However, men don't get off lightly, as the same researchers found they're more likely to have a flawed version of a gene implicated in craving sugary and fatty foods. It's a complicated picture but the key message to take out of this is that if you can't get into your jeans from last year it's never a good idea to blame it on your genes.

It's not just our genes that get the blame for our poor eating habits and expanding waistlines. Nutritionists from the British Nutrition Foundation identified more than 100 reasons people give as to why they find traditional dieting difficult. It's easier to make the excuses than to stick to good eating habits.

The key message is this: the majority of people would find eating well a lot easier if they were dealing with their emotions and not emotionally eating. Turning around your love–hate affair with food into an emotionally healthy relationship is the key.

Remember these positive and important food-related points:

*   Food is not your enemy. It isn't evil and it's important to recognise this.
*   Food is there to enjoy and to sustain your energy and health.
*   When you feel torn over your eating habits it is about your emotions, not food. The aim is to be able to relax while you enjoy food for the right reasons.
*   When you are managing your emotions you can allow yourself a daily or occasional treat, because food can be fun. It's okay to have a treat, but a treat means just that. It's not multiple snacks and it's not a triple helping of ice cream.
*   You are allowed to slip up! No one is perfect. You can't be a superhero; that person doesn't exist. The more you feel you have to be perfect the tougher you are on your emotions and the more likely you're going to run for a snack you don't need.

As I said at the top of this chapter, the things we love, like good food, can become the things we hate because we've been using it destructively and for the wrong reasons.

CHAPTER 6

Feel Good About Yourself to Build a Good Relationship with Food

Comfort yourself so you don't seek out comfort food

If we all had the perfect parents, we would all know how to comfort and soothe ourselves as we go through life. They would have taught us from an early age about the importance of nurturing our confidence, self-esteem and self-acceptance, plus knowing how to handle the difficulties we all face.

But our parents are no more perfect than we are and so many of us struggle with feeling good enough about ourselves. Of course, when you're not feeling good enough to handle your emotions then emotional eating is one way to supposedly comfort yourself.

I think you and I can agree that emotional eating never comforts your heart and soul. It temporarily appears to give you a chemical-induced buzz, fills your stomach and seems to meet a certain need. In reality it just complicates the feelings that need managing through the classic emotional eating 'triangle'—you go through difficult feelings that you don't manage, you then emotionally eat and that emotional eating leads you to feeling worse.

DISSECTING COMPLEX EMOTIONS

Life can be best thought of as one long learning process. No one knows it all and, particularly when it comes to our emotional life, we are always learning. I believe strongly in what I call the 'truthful path', where you know you're on a continuous journey. You never get complacent about your self-knowledge and knowledge of others. You don't let pride get in the way of having good, honest dealings with the world. And you don't get lazy thinking you've been there, done that and you have life 'sorted'. That's when the most surprising things rear up with their ugly, unexpected heads and bite you.

One way to stay on this truthful path is through acknowledging how complex we are as humans, especially regarding our emotional life. If it was simply the case that you argued with your partner and the issue was as plain as day, then you wouldn't be emotional eating. But even a simple disagreement with our partner can set alight so many different emotions within us. The echoes and dark clouds of past difficulties hang over present difficulties. For instance, when you argue with your partner it may automatically bring up a sense of rejection. This may be due to your parents rejecting you when you tried to argue a point growing up. This sense of rejection that surfaces in a disagreement with your partner is profound and far from simple.

Thomas's emotional eating experience

Thomas, 39, is a friend who works in the media and who confided in his friends after a breakup with his now ex-partner that she had been mentally and physically abusive for the last couple of years of their four-year relationship. His friends were appalled that he'd kept this hidden and hadn't confided in anyone.

When he finally came clean about this, he explained that he had felt a huge amount of shame and worthlessness during the relationship. Thomas had been emasculated by his ex-partner's behaviour and strongly believed that a 'real' man would have never been abused. This strongly-held belief about what is and isn't masculine meant he kept his silence. But that silence was so painful he turned to emotional eating.

When we first became friends, Thomas struck me, and others, as a fit, healthy and confident man getting on with life and enjoying it to the full. Within a couple years of this relationship starting he had begun to gain weight rapidly. You don't judge your friends and although it was a noticeable weight gain of probably eight or so kilograms, it didn't occur to me, even in my line of work, that he was harbouring such emotional pain over his relationship. Thomas had developed a very good façade of happiness that fooled everyone.

Emotional energiser solution: Thankfully Thomas had an epiphany when he realised he had to get out of his relationship. He accepted he could not change his partner's abusive behaviour and knew he should never have put up with this treatment. I told him how happy it made me that he'd realised the solution to his feelings of depression and anger over the relationship, and subsequent emotional eating, was to get out and heal from this experience. He explained that part of his self-induced epiphany was waking up to the reality that if she became pregnant he would be tied to her for the rest of his life, as he's a deeply responsible and loyal sort of person. The thought of having a baby with someone and then divorcing them went against the grain of his nature.

Trigger identification: Because Thomas turned his life around on his own before admitting to friends what he'd been through, he hadn't consciously considered the triggers that sent him to comfort food. When we discussed what had gone on, it seemed that not only was his emotional eating triggered when she yelled at him or slapped his face, but also simply the journey home from work served as a trigger. Thomas's anxiety mounted on his journey home as he wondered what mood she'd be in. During the day, if her name came up on his mobile, his stomach would lurch, again with feelings of fear that she might want to have an argument. These were the times he grabbed that extra couple of bags of crisps and other snacks to soothe his anxiety.

Trigger tips: Getting out of this abusive relationship was the fantastic starting point for Thomas learning that he shouldn't feel he has to hide difficulties from his good friends. He recognised that although he had apparently had 'good enough' confidence before getting into this relationship that it actually couldn't have been that strong. Why else would he have let the abuse escalate from her undermining him, to her calling him foul names and then eventually to her slapping and hitting him?

By working on his confidence Thomas is feeling much better about the entire experience, healing from it and moving forward. He's on top of his emotional eating because he now understands the importance of facing even the most challenging situations.

Where, during that damaging relationship Thomas turned to heaped plates of rich, savoury comfort food (sweet things were not his comfort food of choice), now those meals are for family occasions.

This is a good time to turn to you and your confidence.

BUILDING YOUR CONFIDENCE SO YOU CAN FACE WHAT LIFE THROWS AT YOU

Having good levels of confidence is essential and will make a huge difference to your entire life and help you overcome emotional eating. There's no magic pill to give you more confidence and as with all of the best things in life it's a day-by-day process to boost yours.

Problems with confidence can originate early in life when parents fail to nurture a child's esteem and they only develop low or even no confidence. Alternatively, some people can be doing quite well in life only to have a major trauma send their confidence plummeting.

Think of confidence as your inner voice that tells you you're doing 'okay', that you can face challenges, that you can respect others but that you also can respect yourself. Confidence is an enormous comfort—it's the best sort of comfort 'food'.

Our confidence levels are not set in stone, as Thomas's story demonstrates. You can be going about your life thinking you're doing well until either one profound, painful experience changes that or someone picks away at your confidence until you're in a damaging relationship, as he was, that you would never have predicted.

These types of experiences have far-reaching effects, not only with damaging your confidence, but also increasing rates of anxiety and depression. Left unchecked, traumas, anxieties and insecurities encourage a vicious downward cycle when it comes to your confidence.

Thankfully, Thomas didn't allow his abusive relationship to become the template for future relationships. But it's all too easy to do that and I've met many people who, after one abusive relationship, think that that's what they should expect in the next relationship. This reflects their low levels of confidence and leads to them completely lowering their expectations.

It's time for you to become your own confidence coach. This is the best long-term solution to keeping your confidence high and increasing your ability to prevent emotional eating. What follows is a vast array of strategies you can start using from today. Some are new strategies and some are strategies I've already mentioned that are worth further emphasis.

Your confidence-coach tips, tricks and techniques

The following tips have all been useful in my life-coaching work and many people who have used them have said they have had great benefits from them. Try all of these, devise your own variations, use what works and leave behind what doesn't (I want you to have the confidence to say, 'That tip she recommended didn't do anything for me.').

*   Begin by letting go of the biggest confidence myth many have that there are 'confident people' versus those who don't have confidence. You might be holding this myth consciously or at a subconscious level. It's damaging to turn confidence into a 'me-and-them' battle. Challenge this thinking and realise that anyone can develop confidence. Plus, the most confident people on the outside might be pretending. Or, if they're genuinely confident at this time, they might lose their confidence in the future.

* I've spoken of that 'little devil on your shoulder' and how easily it starts chattering, especially when it comes to your confidence. It may tell you that you're useless, you'll never get any better, you just don't have what it takes, or other negative talk. Such thinking becomes a habit and must be challenged. Research found a 10–15 per cent improvement in confidence when people think more positively.
* Keep challenging yourself to develop a cup-half-full attitude by focusing on the positives in your day. It's so easy to throw in the emotional towel and have a cup-half-empty or even completely empty approach to life. When you think like this it can become a self-fulfilling prophecy. You can choose to find the negatives in daily life, but finding the silver lining boosts your confidence.
* Stop living with 'if onlys' like, 'If only I was six kilograms lighter my partner would love me more and we wouldn't argue so often'. Learn to live in the real world and not a fantasy 'if only' world. If you have an issue with your partner, face it, and don't make inappropriate excuses such as that is it about your weight. You're far more likely to lose excess weight if you're not blaming things on your weight. Looking at issues honestly and handling the emotions around them is far more constructive.
* Trust your intuition! The most confident people tell me they are guided by their gut feeling. They believe in what their intuition (think of your intuition as a sixth sense) is telling them about the situation. You would be surprised at how much all your senses acting together pick up on, for example, another person's body language and subtle intentions. Stop doubting decisions you make, accept your intuition is good and it will help you take a major step to higher confidence. Those riddled with doubts about life events such as leaving an unhappy relationship never trust in their intuition when it's telling them: do it, go for it, believe what I'm saying!

* Build your confidence and improve your emotional eating by expecting more from others. Do people in your life talk the talk but then don't walk the walk? For instance, so many unhappy relationships are due to people listening to the words that a neglectful, thoughtless, or even abusive partner says about changing, but then not looking at their behaviour. Did they really change their behaviour in line with the words they told you? Or was their talk cheap and as a result you have been lured into staying in a damaging relationship longer? The rule should be that if someone doesn't do as they say, you tackle them on it. I've used romantic relationships as an example but I'm sure you know this applies to all your interactions.

* Try feel-good tricks like singing your own anthem (a song that you love and that lifts or inspires you). You can sing it to yourself when you're at work or in public and are feeling stressed and ready to head to the nearest fast-food joint. Keep your favourite uplifting songs on your MP3 player, because it's amazing how rousing tunes can lift you to a better emotional place.

* Visualisations can be very helpful in moments of emotional turmoil. When you're feeling negative, visualise a happy memory. Actually close your eyes for a moment and remember all the details of that time and place and the happiness it gave you. These visualisations can help you get into a better emotional place to deal with the negative feelings.

* Confident people accept that failure is a part of life and is absolutely fine. In fact, failure can be positive because it helps you look at solutions—and finding solutions builds confidence. I once heard someone use the saying that mistakes are simply 'miss-takes'— and it's so true. You need to do another 'take', just as they do in the movie business. This is especially true when you're moving out of your comfort zone and trying to deal with emotions. If you've tried something when it came to, for example, communicating

over an issue, and it didn't work, you're not a failure! You're far from a failure because you had the confidence to put yourself out there. At least you've learned something. When you look at so-called failures in these terms as opposed to believing that a failure makes you a failure, it helps prevent emotional eating.

* Develop a new interest or skill that will help create a new confident frame of mind and make you realise that you can be a 'doer'. You're not going to sit at the window watching the world go by—you're going to be part of it. So think through what you need to do to achieve this step by step. Make a 'to do' list. For example, research local colleges for evening classes. Make a decision about which one is best and how to apply. Using manageable steps, you'll reach your goal—building confidence.

* Start prioritising your life. Many who lack confidence try to do 'it all' and then don't do anything well as they're not very good at prioritising. Build as much enjoyment as possible into your lifestyle. Do the necessary chores, don't worry about the rest and prioritise all-important time for the wonderful you.

* I have mentioned picking up the phone to people when you're in crisis or when you need to just put aside what you're dealing with for the moment. But it's not always about you when you phone someone. We regularly hide sentimental feelings, often because of a fear our sentiments will be rejected. But telling people good things—phoning them to say how much they mean to us—makes them feel good and boosts our confidence that we can relate better. This is a good way to use your intuition. Think about a person you care about and who cares for you—maybe a relation or a friend—who perhaps you haven't said anything nice to for a while. Make today the day you do so. The wonderful spinoff for you is you'll feel good afterwards and be far less likely to go looking for a snack.

* Try what I call the 'time tunnel technique'. I mentioned focusing on today, the present, in chapter 3 when talking about how we can't change the past—but what can be helpful to any lingering longings and the desire to change the past is being 'mindful' of the younger you. If you could go back in a time tunnel what message would you give to your younger self? What important information that you know now would you tell the younger you? Write it down here and start living by what you'd tell yourself then, from today!
* Confident people realise that they're entitled to leisure time, relaxation, some fun and treats. Allow yourself a daily 'treat' where you do something just for yourself. It might be something as simple as sitting down with your favourite magazine, getting some hobby items sorted out, or going for a walk in the sunshine.
* Finally, accept that the emotional eater inside of you needs love. Finding love, loving yourself and nurturing love, through romantic relationships, friendships and improved family relationships is an important key to gaining confidence in yourself.

Your physical self, confidence and emotional eating

Having general confidence and body confidence is a real issue for so many. One major survey I was involved with found that 64 per cent of women fret about their bodies regularly. How many of those women then emotionally eat to soothe these fretful feelings?

The fact that you emotionally eat and have probably tried numerous diets or other weight-loss methods suggests you have worries around your physical self. These worries may be justified in that you do emotionally eat, you're carrying excess weight and don't have the energy and zest for life that you'd like to. However, these worries may be unjustified and I'd like to stress again that if you have any issues with restricting food, borderline or full-blown anorexia or other such serious problems that you seek professional help as soon as possible.

For most people, thankfully, their emotional eating doesn't take them into the realm of seriously threatening their health. However, it frequently takes them into the realm of having a negative body image. While you're learning to conquer emotional eating, here are a few tips to boost how you feel about your physical self:

*   Always emphasise the one physical attribute you love about yourself. Come on, don't tell me you don't like any of your attributes! For instance, maybe deep down you know that your eyes or your smile are lovely. Don't be modest—focus on that one attribute when you think of your physical self. Keep in mind you have an attribute that you are happy with and can let shine through—like your beautiful smile.

*   No matter whether you're perfectly happy with your weight and shape or you're working on losing excess weight, what you wear can certainly boost your feelings about your body image. It's worth it taking the time to find the look that suits you and makes you feel confident. Play around with different styles and look for ones that emphasise your best points. You can then get dressed and forget about it as you stride out to face your day.

*   Except for one or two mirrors (probably at your dressing table or bathroom—wherever you get ready) take down other mirrors in your home so that you stop focusing on the way you look. It's all too easy when you're struggling with emotional eating, and feeling overweight, to check yourself in every mirror and at every angle—something that has a negative impact on your body confidence.

*   Wisdom comes with age, but you can wise up now and stop buying into the pressure to look perfect. Fun and laughter are more important than worrying about every lump and bump. Hang on to this thought when you start fretting about any lumps and bumps.

THAT OTHER BIG 'C' WORD: COMMUNICATION

It's an absolute truth that relating well to others boosts confidence and diminishes emotional eating. When you feel connected to others you not only improve your wellbeing and confidence, but you handle emotions better. Developing better communication with loved ones and others, like people at work, is a key part of enhancing your feelings of connection. There are numerous ways you can enhance communication and improve your relationships and confidence. Here are some simple tips to try:

* Always think of the clearest way to make a point. People hear more of what you say if you're not beating around the bush. Forget your inner voice saying you have to be apologetic for what you're saying. You don't, you just have to be respectful and straightforward.

* If you know you're going into a situation where effective communication will make all the difference then practise what you need to say. Even rehearse it out loud and think about the effect your words will have.

* Become the best possible listener. Listen to other people's point of view and with your clarity (from the tips above) you're much more likely to find compromise.

* Use empathy when trying to understand what someone is saying. With a sense of purpose, honestly look at an issue from someone else's point of view. Your confidence will surge because you'll realise how much better you can communicate when you understand them.

* Encourage the person you're communicating with by letting them know you care about their point of view and that you want to work things out.

* 'Own' what you're saying. You can do this by using 'I' statements. These are straightforward statements beginning with 'I' as in, 'I think we get on best when we do X, Y and Z'.

* Get practical with your communication. When approaching

a serious issue, choose your time wisely, check how much alcohol they might have had and make sure you haven't had more than a drink or two. Also choose one goal to raise rather than the scattergun effect of bringing up every single issue between you.

* Find your voice and share your opinions. Confident people are happy to have different opinions to others. They learn to express their views without arguing. Start small and mention your favourite TV show when chatting with colleagues at work. As you gain confidence to communicate your views, you'll be able to do so over bigger topics.

* Be hopeful when discussing an issue. By being hopeful and entering a discussion with a positive attitude, your partner is more likely to feel hopeful about the issue.

These tips help enormously in preventing emotional eating because you will know you can communicate clearly and effectively with a variety of people.

RELATE WELL, BOOST CONFIDENCE AND EAT WELL

When it comes to those I have interviewed about emotional eating, probably the biggest issue that sends them running for comfort food is difficulties with people they love. Every relationship goes through ups and downs, with both partners vying for attention, love and even power.

The emotionally-wise couple realise that at any given point the couple, or one of the partners, may have needs or issues that are difficult to meet. This is when the unwise couple ends up arguing in destructive ways. They pull apart, especially when one person has more needs at that time than the other. The wise couple works it out without diminishing each other or their relationship.

Relationships are also about compromise. From the outside that might appear to mean that every partner gives something up when in a relationship. However, by viewing the bigger picture, each partner should feel that they're benefiting more by compromising with each other. The people I have met who have the happiest relationships with food have happier relationships with others. They realise they're in it together and that compromise and communication enhances them as individuals and as a couple.

When you face an issue with your partner you will feel so much better about your relationship and yourself when you resolve it through discussion and perhaps compromise—it may not have been perfect but you got there in the end. You're far less likely to sneak off seeking comfort from food when you know your relationship is a safe haven.

PREVENTION IS BETTER THAN CURE

Here comes another mention of those 'if onlys'. You might think that if you had only been thinking along the lines of the EED over the years that you may not be an emotional eater. Yes, of course prevention is better than cure but to start down the right path now is fantastic. Pledge to yourself that from today you can start preventing the common mistakes that cause heartache and end up in emotional eating.

The following are what I would call damage limitation tips to help you in romantic relationships. They can also be applied to most relationships, from work to family to friendships. These help you handle your emotions in such a way that you're less likely to comfort eat:

* Don't stew over things. If you can't get an issue out of your mind and if you're working yourself up over it and you can't seem to rationalise it or let it go, then you need to talk about it with your partner. Do this before it boils over into a problem for you both, as well as snacking for you.

* Having said that, if it's a small issue that's not really playing on your mind, ask yourself how you would feel if your partner raised a similar issue with you? Would you be fine with it or

think it was petty? If you would feel it was petty then remind yourself about the bigger picture.

* Start making regular discussions—or relationship check-ups as I call them—a part of the way you relate to each other. When you're both relaxed, discuss what's going right between you as well as potential relationship triggers. Again, these last three strategies help make your relationship feel more like a safe haven. When you're feeling safe you don't need comfort from food.

* Make a point to remind yourself every day why you first fell in love. It's easy to forget these important things with the daily grind of life. But did you fall in love because they were the funniest, kindest person you had ever met? After month in, month out, and year in, year out of stresses and strains, you might forget that. Hold that close in your heart.

* Accept responsibility for your part of the relationship. You can't expect your partner to always make you feel better, always help you de-stress and always help you find solutions to your problems. Growing emotionally means you accept emotional responsibility in relationships.

* Think through, when you're calm, the pattern your arguing may form. I've already discussed how so much of our behaviour is about 'habits', and arguing can be habitual. Plan how you can move forward on any patterns you identify.

* There's nothing wrong with a couple agreeing that some topics are off-limits because you just may never compromise. Essentially you both can agree to disagree.

* Remember what I said about mistakes? They are there to learn from! It's no good resolving an issue but then falling back into the same negative cycle. Agree that you will check with each other on how you're both doing with particular issues. You can ask each other in a positive manner, 'How am I doing with X, Y or Z?' Remember, lots of praise before you discuss any negative feedback if they aren't doing so well on X, Y or Z.

* Learn to ask for the love you need. For example, if you need extra TLC because your manager's giving you a hard time at work, ask your partner for it. Even the most loving partner may not realise when things have got worse in a particular situation for you. Never expect your partner or anyone else to be a mind reader. Even if they've known you for years they may have other things on their mind and assume you're okay if you haven't said otherwise.

ANGER, COMMUNICATION AND EMOTIONAL EATING

In the previous chapter we took a closer look at your emotional eating profile and I highlighted the emotion of anger and its part in emotional eating. Communicating your anger is crucial to preventing emotional eating. Anger is equal in power to hurtful feelings in the part it plays in using comfort food. If you end up arguing due to your anger, here are key tips to use in the heat of the moment:

* Angry people don't listen, so give each other two minutes of uninterrupted talking time. Use a timer on your phone, or even an egg timer, if needs be to stick to this.
* Agree if things get too heated you'll take a 'breather' and then try discussing the issue from a different angle. Many issues are not resolved in one go.
* Resist throwing an irrelevant issue into an already heated exchange. It's easy to throw in something that annoys your partner just to wind up the situation. For instance, throwing in the fact that their best friend is a bit of a joker when you're actually arguing about showing more respect to each other lessens your chance of resolving the issue. Avoid bringing up irrelevant things and stick to whatever you're disagreeing about.
* If an argument is escalating, count to ten before raising your voice. This actually gives your brain a chance to get in gear rather than be dominated by strong emotions. If it doesn't

work let your partner know you must leave the room to cool down because you don't want to say anything you'll regret.

* Avoid making sweeping generalisations like, 'you never help me!' It's very rare that someone never does something or always does something negative. You might find your partner thinks, "Well if they think I never help then why start now?".

* Mind your language and instead of shouting something awful, e.g., 'You f**king bas***d', think of something funny to shout like, 'You silly bunny!' to dispel anger. It can work and you're far less likely to regret it. Regrets frequently lead to comfort snacking to soothe that difficult emotion.

* 'Don't let the sun go down on anger' might be an old adage, but it is true. It's far better to make up before bedtime or at least to give each other a hug, and the reassurance that you'll work it out, and suggest continuing at another time. People tell me when they haven't made up they head to the kitchen for emotional eating, and that's true at any time of day.

* Another behaviour bound to cause regret is when you're angry and you go for your partner's known emotional jugular vein. If you've been with someone a while, you're bound to know what really hurts them. Check yourself before hitting them below the belt. Also, don't make threats you don't want to follow through, such as saying, 'we should get a divorce!' Once you put the D-word into your arguments it's a very slippery slope to actually getting one.

All of these tips can help you manage angry situations better. They're practical and grounded, which is why they're important to keep in mind. What happens when we're angry is that our emotions take over and we forget until it's too late how much damage we do to our partners and ourselves. You don't want this damage playing out in the triangle of emotional eating.

Pride has a place to play in your relationship as it's a powerful, usually difficult emotion that, left unchecked, is responsible for much of your emotional eating. Ultimately, when you've expressed yourself, listened to your partner and hopefully understood each other you will enhance your relationship.

It's always far more important to be happy together than for one of you to be right about something. Pride equals wanting to be right in these circumstances. Someone can be the most right person in the world—and the loneliest—having lost out in love by never graciously bowing out of an argument that might not even have been worth having.

SELF-ACCEPTANCE AND EMOTIONAL EATING

Self-acceptance is crucial in preventing emotional eating. Self-acceptance is a journey we must all go on. It is rare to find someone who, fully, or almost fully, accepts themselves. A theme throughout the EED is the fact that many people are far too critical of themselves, and this cuts across various personality traits.

The outgoing person might wonder if they're actually acceptable and likable if they've taken over a social event with their personality. They may worry that others found them too much or felt they couldn't get a word in edgeways. The shy introvert might feel the same way except for the opposite reason: they don't accept themselves and so they're self-critical, thinking along the lines of 'why can't I be more outgoing?'.

Self-acceptance helps us manage feelings of guilt and regret. You're kinder and gentler on yourself when you accept yourself because doing so means we accept that we all make mistakes, we all face issues and we're no better or worse than anyone else.

These sorts of positive feelings are powerful protectors against suffering excessive guilt over things like mistakes. Self-acceptance also makes it less likely your pride will get in the way when you know you should back down. Because we know, through self-acceptance, that those sorts of things really don't matter. When we accept ourselves we subsequently are far less likely to emotionally eat.

Developing your self-acceptance plays right out across your life, from your romantic relationships to every other relationship. Why not begin by reminding yourself here of what you like about yourself?:

_____

_____

_____

_____

_____

_____

_____

_____

_____

_____

_____

_____

_____

_____

_____

_____

_____

_____

_____

_____

_____

_____

_____

_____

_____

_____

_____

_____

_____

Now make a note of the last time you were beating yourself up emotionally for having, for example, made a mistake and headed straight for a snack food:

_____

_____

_____

_____

_____

_____

_____

_____

_____

_____

_____

_____

_____

_____

THE 'DISEASE TO PLEASE' AND YOUR EMOTIONAL EATING

A big stumbling block to self-acceptance is the so-called 'disease to please'. This is where you feel you must please others, often at some cost to yourself, or, in more extreme cases, no matter the cost to yourself. Again, this is a trait that cuts across all personalities and situations. If you feel compelled to always say yes to people's requests of you—even if it's inconvenient or you feel taken advantage of—that is one of the key signs.

People with the disease to please do so in many ways: by constantly going out of their way to do favours for others. At the bottom of this is the misguided belief that unless they please others they aren't likable enough.

As with other ways of not putting enough emphasis on your emotional life or wellbeing, when you're pleasing everyone else it leaves you with very little inside. You simply don't have the emotional sustenance to handle stresses and strains. And what does this mean? Of course, you guessed it, and you may well have done it—you turn to food for some emotional relief.

Use the crucial disease to please list to ease emotional eating:

* Accept yourself!
* Be helpful within reason.
* Practise saying no to requests that go beyond the call of duty.
* Ask others for help when you need it.
* Delegate tasks at work if it's your responsibility to do so.
* Combat feelings that to be liked you have to always say yes.
* When you slip backwards, for example saying yes to something that causes you stress or puts you out, you can change your mind!
* Recognise those who take advantage of your 'pleasing' nature.
* Finally, when you stretch yourself too thin because you've gone backwards with your disease to please, be vigilant about not emotionally eating.

I hope this chapter has given you lots of strategies to move forward about feeling good about yourself, feeling more confident, being able to communicate and fighting urges to be a people pleaser.

We now move on to boosting your mood in order to boost your ability to avoid emotional eating and to help lose excess weight

CHAPTER 7

Boost Your Mood for a Better Weight

Guide your mood to a better place so you are the guide of your emotions

I hope you've now come a long way in understanding how the various strands of your personality, your past and how you handle your emotions and your experiences all interweave to influence your relationship with food. It's amazing to think of all these parts of ourself and our life weaving together. This is such a dynamic process and you need to understand you can be the master or mistress of this process.

We now turn to mood, and the various ways you can boost your mood in order to gain control of emotional eating. Think of your mood as you would the waters of the ocean across our planet. Sometimes there are gentle waves, barely moving, tranquil and peaceful. Other times there are huge, crashing, violent-type surges of water that are extreme and powerful.

There are so many ways to handle and understand our mood states, to manage them when they seem like surging out of control and to lift them up when they crash down. Let's look at some of these areas in your quest to manage your mood and manage your emotional eating.

IMPROVE YOUR SELF-CARE AND IMPROVE EMOTIONAL EATING

To help put you into a mood-boosting mindset we need to explore the important area of self-care. Self-care behaviours are the opposite of self-destructive behaviours. We can all think of many, classic self-destructive behaviours and they include: drinking too much, abusing drugs, smoking, allowing people to abuse us, inappropriate relationships and sexual behaviour, never meeting deadlines, not fulfilling our obligations to others, and many other similar destructive behaviours. Of course, emotional eating can be self-destructive behaviour. It's self-destructive in that you avoid learning to cope with the challenging emotions we all must cope with. It also leads to excessive weight gain, which isn't good for your health or wellbeing.

Self-care means you feel good enough about yourself to care for your own needs. Meeting your basic needs is absolutely crucial for your wellbeing and mood state. Self-care is about many things including learning how to express your emotions so that you keep everything else in check, such as your eating habits.

The foundations of self-care

The whole premise of self-care is to provide yourself with a solid foundation on which to live your life in a way that you can cope with your emotions and keep your mood state in good shape. The key areas include the basics of getting enough good quality sleep—absolutely vital to emotional wellbeing. Then, of course, there's finding balance in your life between various demands like relationships and work, not drinking excessively and not taking drugs, stopping bad habits like smoking, expressing your needs to others and, of course, eating well to fuel your energy needs.

Sleep hygiene for self-care

It is crucial that you get enough sleep because when you have done so you can meet the demands of your waking life so much better. I'm sure you know how great you feel when you've had a good night's sleep and there are many tips coming up to help you get this regularly. Not only do you generally feel better and are able to meet the demands of your day when you sleep well, but a study found that sticking to regular sleeping patterns helps women, at least, keep excess weight off.

YOUR GUIDE TO A HEAVENLY NIGHT'S SLEEP

An important consideration is your body's own natural circadian rhythm. Our evolutionary heritage is to go to bed with the sunset and rise with sun up. But this is complicated by our modern lifestyles. Also, there's evidence that some people do better with shorter sleep-and-rest cycles. It's important to recognise this diversity in sleep patterns and find what works best for you. Unfortunately, there's some evidence from the University of Zurich that you partly inherit a propensity to sleep well and deeply, or not so well and lightly.

The following are a number of sleep strategies to try, all of which will improve your mood and help you face emotional eating. Most are based on sleep hygiene research and others are from my own and clients' experiences of being light sleepers.

You and your overall lifestyle

What you do when awake impacts tremendously on the quality of your sleep, so give honest answers to the following:

*   How much stress is in your life? General stress is a major culprit for keeping you awake worrying. I'm tackling de-stressing tips in the next chapter on metabolism boosters, which will be important for you to put into action, as excess stress makes us

sluggish. You'll improve your sleep cycle as you eliminate stress.

* How much caffeine do you drink? Research confirms caffeine after 3 p.m. impacts negatively on sleep even if your bedtime is, for example, 11 p.m. Substitute caffeinated teas/coffees/soft drinks with decaf or herbal drinks.

* Do you enjoy alcohol? There is nothing wrong with a little tipple but drinking any more than a couple of units of alcohol is significantly more likely to have a disruptive effect on your sleep. Many emotional eaters confide in me that they drink alcohol at night to help them relax over the emotional turmoil they have bubbling inside them.

* What foods do you eat? Quite apart from thinking about emotional eating, if you love hot and spicy cuisine you need to wise up to things like chilli, onions and garlic over-stimulating your circulation. Better to have these at lunchtime and after 7 p.m. choose foods with soporific qualities like turkey or salmon, low GI foods like oats, wholegrain pastas, lentil dishes and even lettuce or banana sandwiches. Unfortunately, the snacks you might turn to as an emotional eater, like processed snack foods, are high in sugar and/or salt—both can frazzle you, making it harder to get off to sleep.

* Do you exercise? If not, choose something you enjoy doing regularly. You might hate the gym but if you love something like dancing you can build dance classes into your routine. Regular exercise promotes wellbeing, which promotes in turn better quality sleep. Be warned, you shouldn't do vigorous exercise within two–three hours of your bedtime because your circulation keeps pumping at a higher rate for a number of hours after vigorous exercise, making sleep difficult.

* Are you a techno junkie? If you love surfing the Net and playing computer games, such focused mental activity increases restlessness and disturbs sleep. The golden rule is to not use such technology at least an hour before bedtime. Also, recent studies suggest that excessive online

usage disturbs mood balance and can lead to a depressed mood state. From what people tell me, they're more likely to emotionally eat when feeling that way.

* Do you love films and television? If you love watching films or TV programmes late at night, ensure they're not action thrillers, full of police chases. These raise adrenalin levels, preventing you from going off to sleep easily.

* Are you an owl or a lark? Some interesting research found that many people are naturally an owl—coming to life later in the day, concentrating better in the afternoon, enjoying a late bedtime and being later to rise. Whereas those who are larks are the opposite—they're early risers, work best in the morning and prefer an earlier bedtime. Although research suggests you can retrain this, most people usually only successfully shift an hour or two one way or the other.

Strategies and steps to take during the day and night

After considering all the questions above, try these strategies, because not only are they good for basic self-care, they will help you sleep better. I can't over-emphasise how a good night's sleep will help fuel your ability to face emotional tension.

We're back to those diaries. If you're really having problems sleeping, keep a sleep diary for a week, making a note of when you get off to sleep, wake up, and take catnaps. Look for any pattern and try to identify why you sleep better or worse at times.

* An hour or so before bedtime take a warm bath or shower—not too hot as this can be over-stimulating. Try using calming aromatherapy oil in the bath. Lavender oil is perfect.

* Read a magazine or book you find relaxing. Follow the same principle as with watching television—reading over-stimulating material will keep you awake.

* It is important to watch TV away from the bedroom. The bedroom should be associated with sleep (and sex!) and not

other activities.

* Try relaxation techniques when lying in bed. Start by clenching then relaxing the major muscle groups, working through each major muscle group one at a time. This will help relax you.

* Next, visualise a restful scene like lying on a tropical beach with warm sunshine on your back and without a care in the world.

* Use deep breathing. Inhale slowly and then exhale to the count of ten. Also use such relaxation techniques during the day when tension is mounting so you prevent it mounting to sleep-disruptive points.

* Relaxation tapes are helpful to some—from whale music to white noise and self-hypnosis tapes, experiment with different ones.

* Ensure the bedroom temperature is balanced between not being too cold or too warm, and also check bedroom lighting.

* Don't use a powerful reading light as this can be over-stimulating. A dimmer switch is ideal for getting the right balance. Some find coloured light bulbs more relaxing.

* Noise levels in the bedroom can disrupt your sleep. Although some could sleep through a train, most have some noise sensitivity. Heavy curtains, draft excluders and earplugs can help.

* Use calming colours in your bedroom like pale shades of blue, pale lavenders and lilacs, often used in mental health units. Pale brick and earth tones and fleshy pinks also promote tranquillity. Deeper greens promote comfort and darker earth tones, dark, fleshy pinks or deep, rich butter tones are also soothing.

* Use a few drops of relaxing aromatherapy oil in your pillow stuffing such as lavender, geranium or sandalwood.

* Put any worries out of your mind. Make a list of 'must-dos' for the next day before you get into bed. Don't think about them for the rest of the night. If stressful thoughts creep in, banish them.

*   Sip relaxing camomile or other 'night remedy' teas. Any evening snacks should again consist of slow-burning carbohydrates. Snacking within thirty minutes of bedtime causes digestive activity keeping you awake.
*   Go on, have some fun in bed. Having satisfying sex will help you sleep by releasing tension.
*   The quality of your mattress and bedding can either promote or inhibit a restful night. Seriously consider investing in a good quality (e.g., pocket sprung) mattress and bedding.
*   Reassure yourself that if you wake early you will cope. Take one night at a time. Worrying that you won't sleep all week won't help.

Consult your doctor if you've tried all of the above and you still sleep poorly. To give yourself a fighting chance with your emotional eating you have to be rested.

LET YOUR GROWING SELF-CARE CONTINUE

Self-care can be the underlying foundation of letting go of your emotional eating. This self-care also encompasses finding a balance in your life. It can be tough enough facing up to emotions but it's even harder to do so when your life balance is out of sync.

Here are a few key pointers to maintaining a good work–life balance:
*   Is the extra work you're doing absolutely necessary?
*   What will happen if you don't do it? Will the sky fall in?
*   If a friend was undertaking the same excess work as you are, would you advise them that they're doing too much? If so, you should follow your own advice.
*   For every half an hour of work you do outside your basic hours, match it with half an hour of self-care.
*   One clear sign your work–life balance is out of kilter is if it's causing trouble in your relationship, isolating you from friends

and causing you stress levels that are too high.

* Test the waters of working less a little bit at a time, for example, if you tend to stay at the office an extra couple of hours each evening, start leaving fifteen minutes earlier for a week, building to half an hour earlier, and so on until you're doing fewer hours.

MOOD-BOOSTING TIPS, TRICKS AND TECHNIQUES

We should all be in the business of uplifting our mood to cope with modern life. When it comes to emotional eating, you enhance your chances to get on top of it when your mood is balanced and lifted.

Everyone needs to find what works for them because your life, your responses to difficult emotions and your subsequent emotional eating is unique to you. Try out the tips below that resonate with you and your situation, and give the others a chance too:

* The best starting point is being kinder to yourself. Treat yourself regularly to the little pleasures of life. After all, we run ourselves ragged looking after others and our career, but rarely show ourselves that kindness. Give yourself five minutes daily to put your feet up and do exactly what you want to do: read your favourite magazine, kick back with a nurturing herbal tea like chamomile or snatch a little snooze.

* The devil on your shoulder has already been mentioned, and it's time to change that negative, voice criticising everything you do to a gentle, positive, little angel. This applies across your entire life and not just your emotional eating. Start telling yourself you're doing well, that you're good enough, or even better, that you're great! You won't always get the praise and compliments you want from others that you're entitled to, so start praising yourself. I usually find it's the loveliest people who are least likely to praise themselves.

* Setting your boundaries, for instance, as Liz did with her work, has a tremendous influence on your mood. Think

116

about this: it's easy to end up being taken for granted or allowing others to treat you poorly when you don't set your boundaries. Feeling taken advantage of so often drives people to emotional eating—they feel hurt and frustrated. Turn that around and set your boundaries, letting others know when they've overstepped the mark. Remember, so much of not setting your own boundaries is about a fear of rejection—back to that disease to please. If ever there was a mood sapper it's this, and ultimately I want you to ask this question daily: if they are going to reject me for simply setting my boundaries, do I need them in my life? These are exactly the sorts of people who ignite your desire to emotionally eat.

* Spread a little mood-lifting happiness by turning your newfound feeling outwards and making others feel good in your company. Remark on someone's new haircut, a new outfit or something they have done well. As I mentioned earlier, it's important to let people know you appreciate their time and company.

* Don't underestimate the power of laughter to boost mood. Research shows that laughter increases the production of endorphins—those feel-good brain chemicals. Why not get a regular dose of your favourite comedy programme, rent a classic comedy film and get out to a comedy club occasionally? You should message or e-mail friends anything that tickles you, as they'll probably appreciate it too. When you've shared laughter it feels so good that it boosts your determination to face other emotions.

* When you learn to embrace spontaneity it helps you throw off habits of the past that mean you stay just the way you are. Staying just the way you are seems safe, but as you know as an emotional eater, it's not really safe. So become a yes person when someone asks you at the last minute to join them going to an event, to grab a film etc. Forget those chores you're planning to do tonight—get out and grab that opportunity.

* Activate change in your environment because, quite frankly, boredom is a mood-killer. Yes, I've said that some of our habits and routines help speed us through the day but activating even small changes wherever it makes sense can boost your mood and help transform you into a 'doer'. The doer you need to become will help you face your emotions. Start small and take a new route to work, visit a new sandwich shop at lunchtime, say hello to that new colleague or shake up your evening and weekend routine.

* Sticking with this theme, let's move on to stimulating your brain. If everything seems a bit lacklustre in your life it will drag your mood down. This situation, left unchecked, has surprising consequences for emotional eating. Research shows that activating new parts of your brain is a natural mood booster. A daily puzzle or crossword can help wipe the cobwebs from your mind. Why not take up a hobby that's a bit challenging, like learning a new language or playing a musical instrument? Or if you don't have time to play an instrument simply meditating to classical music can soothe an overstressed mind, leaving you ready to fight stresses and eat well. Satisfy your brain's natural need to learn—with surprising results.

* Often, a great starting point to lifting your mood is taking very practical steps, and that includes freshening up your look. Go on, try a new hairstyle, new makeup or fashion style. If you're a woman on a budget you can freshen up your look by getting a free make-up makeover at any good beauty counter at a major department store. Relish your new look and enjoy being spoiled for a few minutes.

* Fuel your mood with mood-boost foods. I've already mentioned (above) a few of the calming foods to have in the evening to help improve sleep issues. But also in the summer we tend to have more salads and fresh vegetables, as well as fruit and fruit-based drinks. In countries like Greece and

Spain these feel-good foods are plentiful and locals eat them every day. If you're not in that kind of climate, do your best to get these oxidant-rich foods from your market. They're good for your health and will lift your mood.

* Get creative when it comes to controlling your thinking to help control your mood. Because once you're more in control of your mood it will help you control impulses to emotionally eat. So, for instance, if you're into music, use your love of music to help you think creatively. Imagine the playlist the 'DJ of your mind' is playing. Is it playing tunes that are negative, self-critical and anxious—or is the music uplifting? It's time to change to mood-boosting mental tunes. Or maybe you're a movie buff. Imagine your mind is creating your own uplifting movie scenes to carry you through the day.

* Get wise when it comes to colour therapy, because the colours you wear definitely influence your mood. Although your inclination may be to slip into dark-coloured clothes to match your mood, and some wear dark colours believing it hides their excess weight, opt for brighter colours instead. The vibrancy of the colours makes a difference to your entire attitude. Even adding a colourful necktie, scarf or accessories to your normal outfits will help give you a buoyant mood, to boost you up to combat emotional eating.

* One of the quickest mood boosts is using your personal photos as therapy. Put family, friends and holiday snaps to good use as the wallpaper on your laptop or your mobile. Once in place, you'll be reminded on a daily basis of these memories. Allow yourself to reflect on them when you're tempted to emotionally eat.

* When changing your life—as you are doing now—always fake it to make it. Take a minute to imagine the most confident you could possibly be. Picture yourself as this newly confident person. Now hold that thought as you walk into a meeting or appointment.

* Lift your body language up to confident proportions. Think good, open posture and dump closed-down, rigid body language. Don't fidget, relax your hands, give good eye contact and smile. Just practise this at home. Look at yourself in the mirror standing tall with your shoulders back, compared to crossing your arms across your chest and shrinking down. Can't you see the difference in how these two opposites could affect your mood?

CHALLENGE YOURSELF IN YOUR CAREER TO ENHANCE YOUR MOOD

I just suggested that, like Liz, you might be working excessive hours because you feel you have to make yourself indispensable, or because it becomes a way of hiding from your emotions when you fall into bed exhausted each night. But think just how much emotional eating springs from stress and lack of satisfaction at work? A vast amount! This is an important question to look at as you move forward, as the average person spends more than half their life at work.

You may not be able to change jobs—that's often a luxury many people can't manage. But at the very least you can give yourself hope and discover and create opportunities in your present job with these few steps:

* Do you dream of changing track? Take advantage of any extra skills training offered at your job or take an evening class for that training.
* What would make your present job better? An obvious starting point is to think through what changes would make your work a positive experience for you? What are the issues at work that cause you to emotionally eat during the day? Can these negative aspects to your job be changed for the better? What suggestions would you put your manager for doing so?

* Have a free-association session to brainstorm ideas to bring you closer to your dream job. For instance, if you dream of being on the stage, take a drama class and see if you're a natural. You might just discover you're brilliant at helping behind the scenes, though. Such experiences can help you decide whether to change directions or to keep your dream as a hobby.
* Some companies allow job swapping for a limited period, such as one day or one week. When you step into someone else's shoes and do their job, you appreciate your colleagues more, plus you learn if there is something else you would prefer doing. If your company doesn't offer this, put it in the company suggestion box as a new learning experience for you and your colleagues.

LOVE AND MOOD

We all need, even crave, love. It goes right to the heart of being human. I can't tell you the lengths people go to in order to find love, keep love or maybe hide from love because it's been so painful for them in the past. But a good loving relationship helps optimise your mood and ultimately what you should aim for is a relationship full of what I call the 3 Rs:

Respect: A relationship where you respect yourself and your partner. The mutual respect means you listen to each other and support each other.

Responsibility: Where you and your partner take responsibility for the parts you play in the happy aspects and the unhappy aspects of your relationship. Relationships aren't a one-way street; it's never helpful to play the blame game when things are going wrong, and you should put your hands up if you are at fault.

Reliability: You have to be able to rely on what your partner says, and likewise they need to be able to rely on you. One thing that's important to everyone, and perhaps especially to emotional eaters, is to know you can count on that person to do as they say they will.

Effectively maintaining your relationships will play a crucial part in maintaining an even mood. This goes across all relationships and is crucial to all relationships, but is most important in romantic relationships where we give over our life and share it with another person. If issues and potential issues are being managed well or well enough, and you feel loving towards each other, it will help you prevent emotional eating.

A few key ways to maintain that mood of love include:

*   Prioritising your partner. Your relationship deserves attention otherwise it is easily relegated to second or third place. Book regular date nights for candlelit dinners. Even if budgeting means you have these dinners at home, dress up as if you're going out on the town. You're more likely to stimulate desire when you have made an effort. Plus, it's comforting to know you care enough about each other to prioritise each other, and that's a good preventative measure for emotional eating.

*   Keep generating that loving feeling with even simple things like going for a romantic walk on a cold day or cuddling up at home together to watch a favourite old film. These help you feel more loving and content. In the summer months when couples take more time out together and get out of their usual routine, these things are easier to do regularly. Taking strolls, having dinners in the sunshine or relaxing in the garden or local park generate warmer feelings.

*   Strolling down memory lane by looking at photographs of when you first met will create a golden glow around you. It makes it easier to remember why you first were attracted to each other and fell in love. Make a point, perhaps on special occasions like your wedding anniversary, to flip through photo albums together. Let these shared moments lift your mood.

* Always remember that your partner is not a mind reader. It is a whole lot easier to ask when you need extra attention or love. Use a loving voice and your partner will be much more receptive to your requests. This creates much better and more balanced moods between the two of you.

FRIENDSHIPS HELP MAINTAIN A POSITIVE MOOD

Friendships are absolutely key—whether we have a romantic partner or not—to maintaining a positive mood. Remember that even friendships need freshening up because they can lose their sparkle if they're neglected. Start nurturing them, let your friends know how much you value them and do new things together. Good friendships give you the confidence to venture out of your comfort zone. They can also be a fantastic sounding board for handling your emotions while you learn to face tricky emotional states.

BOOST YOURSELF AND YOUR MOOD WITH GOOD EATING HABITS

Chapter 1 provided you with basic, sound nutritional advice. Now I hope you're understanding yourself better and this understanding leads you to eating habits that fuel your needs and don't make you feel bad about yourself. Here are a few strategies to help you instill good eating habits, remembering that good eating habits help balance your mood:

* Establish a good routine at home and at work when it comes to mealtimes, because chaos at home or work means that your eating is more likely to be chaotic. Also, chaos in your outer world leads to more chaotic emotions within you. This can lead to emotional eating.
* Never underestimate the power of having a good routine throughout your life—not just at mealtimes—to provide you with comfort. This doesn't mean that everything has to be a

habit, but just that generally you know you can get through the demands of your life because things are organised when it comes to the most basic chores like keeping your home tidy or work clothes ready for the week.

* That said, approach your routine with flexibility. It's no good panicking if a crisis happens at work and you have to go in early or leave late, meaning that the routine you're trying to instill gets out of sync. These things are never worth worrying about! Worrying means you're likely to reach for a comforting snack.

* Never shop when hungry, as you're far more likely to grab some comfort food to eat the minute you leave the store. By organising your routine, you can also organise when the optimal time is to do your food shopping.

* Work out what's best for you when it comes to whether you're a three-meals-a-day person or the sort of person who does better on four or five smaller meals. Personally, I need to fuel my needs more frequently and have found that four or five smaller meals mean I'm far less likely to want a snack.

* All snacks aren't bad and if you find you do need more frequent, smaller meals, sometimes a large, healthy snack works as one of those. Stock your cupboards with healthy snacks for when you're allowed such a snack.

* As far as possible, sit down with family members or friends for as many meals per week as possible. This is sadly something that is being lost as the pace of our life has changed. It's never too late to instigate family mealtimes again. Sharing meals and giving each other that little bit of time is certainly a fantastic mood booster.

* Outside of mealtimes always think before you eat, asking yourself whether you are really hungry or whether you are reaching for food as an emotional eating habit—a habit where you're used to just picking up a snack at 10:30 a.m. even when you're not hungry.

The healing from emotional eating will continue as you continue to boost your mood. These ideas are for life and not just for now while you're changing your life. The tips above that resonate with your life and can work for you should be kept in your life from now on.

CHAPTER 8

Metabolism Boosters to Kick-start Your Energy

Energise your metabolism to energise your life

I wouldn't be surprised if you told me you feel sluggish much of the time. I wouldn't be surprised because emotional eaters struggle with two major elements in life: handling difficult emotions and fuelling their energy needs with the appropriate food. These two key elements together—eating well and handling our emotions well—give us a sense of equilibrium. When we have that, we have the emotional and physical energy to get through our life in the most positive way possible.

Don't we already know this from our own experiences with emotional eating? I clearly recall feeling far from energetic when I went through that difficult time in my second pregnancy. My metabolism was sluggish—not energised—and that was an absolute reflection of not facing head-on my difficult emotional life and my emotional eating of snack foods. Together these were draining me. After all, if your inner emotions are in turmoil and you're not managing them, and you feel you're unable to face people with certain things or to strike out and become the confident person you long to be, it drains and depletes your energy. As you turn things around you'll find new energy and a smooth-functioning metabolism. This increased energy will feel fantastic!

In brief, metabolism is the chemical processes that occur within us and any living organism in order to maintain life. These processes are kept in balance in various ways including by what we fuel our bodies with. For instance, if you're a coffee drinker you'll know how that first steaming hot mug of the day gives you an instant boost—essentially speeding up your metabolism with caffeine. But haven't all caffeine drinkers made the mistake of having one or two mugs too many? It can be an unpleasant feeling of being on edge, and that's your chemical processes being put out of balance by too much caffeine.

Metabolism, of course, is influenced by many other things, like physical exercise—after you've had a swim or dashed for a bus you can feel your heart beating more quickly and your metabolism turning over. And below you'll find many metabolism boosters to help lift you out of feeling sluggish.

But also you may have an overactive metabolism from things like drinking too much caffeine and emotionally eating sugary foods that you think will soothe you but actually disturb your metabolism. Once you've had lots of sugary foods, the emotional reaction to that is a feeling of stress. Many of the suggestions to follow will help to balance these things, helping to diminish stress and stressful feelings.

However, it's important to note that sometimes metabolism is affected by a medical issue such as those related to the thyroid. So if you have any concerns about feelings of sluggishness or other physical symptoms, pay a visit to your healthcare provider to have them checked out.

I like to think of metabolism in this analogy of a river. If that river is unpolluted (by poor-quality comfort and junk food) and doesn't have big rocky obstructions (those difficult emotions that emotional eaters try to avoid), it's smooth flowing and full of life, energising you to meet your needs.

If we think of it, it is the natural order of things for us humans to be energetic. Of course, those energy requirements need to be supplied by good eating habits.

It is also an equally important part of our wellbeing for us to balance and manage our emotions, no matter how tricky. Once upon a time life might have been tough without our modern luxuries, but it was more straightforward, as individuals and their communities shared the goal of working side by side for mutual survival. People's emotional lives were equally more straightforward. People simply didn't have untold options of how to spend their time or to choose to leave relationships sometimes at the drop of a hat, as people do nowadays. They lived where they lived without worrying about all the other places they might choose to live; they had their job and didn't worry about applying for dozens of others. They certainly didn't have a choice of 50 varieties of cereal to buy in the supermarket.

Our lives now are far more complicated, and these complications bring more complicated emotions—and more emotional eating. Ultimately, keeping aware of boosting your metabolism is a positive, upwards cycle. Because as you boost your metabolism you energise yourself, and once you're energised you will feel better able to manage emotions. In turn, you will have the motivation to keep your metabolism boosted. Of course, there is the added benefit that this cycle will help you maintain a healthy weight.

FACING THE BIGGEST METABOLISM SAPPER OF ALL

There are many different suggestions for metabolism boosters coming up. But let's start with the biggest metabolism sapper of all apart from illness and medical problems—although, if not tackled, it can lead to both of these. I'm talking stress: a word applying to a vast array of issues and events, like feeling stressed about going on a first date, going for a job interview or moving house. These three examples aren't related in the slightest, but stress is the common strand between them. It's absolutely crucial to understand and manage your stress because it sends your metabolism out of kilter, sapping your energy to face your emotional eating. When your metabolism needs boosting to energise you, stress does the opposite.

The concept of stress is misleading because what one person claims is stress simply might not faze another. You might find the stress of deadlines sends you into an emotional eating spin, but someone else might thrive on deadlines. However, we all understand when someone talks about stress that it's a general feeling of being pressured, out of control and/or overwhelmed—put simply, it's an unpleasant mood state.

Of course, stress is a natural mood state, and it's important to understand that. An optimum level of low-to-medium stress keeps you on your toes and ensures you do your best. For example: putting your best foot forward on a date, being confident at a job interview and managing all that moving house entails. A little bit of stress is a good signal telling you that you had better ratchet-up your performance at whatever you're facing. Most people handle this type of stress fairly easily. Although as an emotional eater even a nominal level of stress may heap added worry onto other emotions you're not handling well and send you looking for comfort food.

Putting aside emotional eating, as stress levels increase above a nominal level, almost everyone finds their coping and performance decreases. There are a few individuals who cope well with any level of stress, but most people struggle to cope when too stressed: they get tongue-tied on that date, or say something 'stupid' at that job interview or end up screaming at their partner during that house move.

When stress levels increase even further, it has a purpose: to signal that you need to take urgent action and/or respond to what's going on in your life. But for many, high levels of stress overwhelm them rather than drive them to taking action.

High stress levels have an enormous impact on emotional eating and the food and feelings triangle then kicks in with a vengeance. This is when your metabolism is stretched to the limit and your energy levels are drained. After a big, stressful, metabolism-damaging episode, the wise thing to do is to plan to do things differently. Instead, again, too many fail to learn from overwhelming and out-of-control stress. If this continues for too long they risk burnout.

In the UK the statistics make ugly reading, with recent government health and safety executive data confirming that nearly half a million workers are suffering full-blown stress-related illnesses. Research from York University in 2009 suggested that 13.5 million working days are lost annually due to stress. Imagine how many of those people are drained of energy and are sitting at home emotionally eating.

Your levels of stress and emotional eating

Because stress affects your whole system, once you get on top of it you will probably find your metabolism seems to operate much more smoothly. You will generally feel better physically and emotionally, plus you will have more energy. You'll be in a far better position to prevent emotional eating. So let's consider stress in more detail before looking at a variety of metabolism boosters.

Look through this symptoms checklist to see if you're experiencing metabolism-sapping stress.

* You have the awful feeling that your metabolism is running on adrenaline.
* You find yourself increasingly dependent on caffeine to keep you going.
* You're finding sleep doesn't come easily—you're either awake for long periods or sleeping in short fits and bursts.
* You feel fidgety and restless and can't even relax when you have a chance to sit down.
* You just feel sluggish and drained of energy.
* You find it hard to concentrate and must re-read pages in a book, or you lose track of the plot in a film.
* You've become short tempered, particularly with your nearest and dearest.
* You feel tearful at times, despite not being a tearful sort of person .

* You might find yourself feeling panicky even, for example, once you've met a deadline.
* You're experiencing physical symptoms of panic like heart palpitations or sweaty palms.
* Your emotional eating has increased.
* You may be drinking more alcohol to relax generally and/or to get a good night's sleep (remember, this is a false type of relaxation).
* If you're a smoker, your level of smoking has increased.
* You lack the desire to do things you usually enjoy (e.g., sports).
* You have an imminent deadline that you're panicking about more than you normally would.
* You feel numb inside and/or that you've got nothing left to give.

Did many of these checklist items resonate with you? Are you surprised at how many seemed familiar? If any ring true, it's important you get on top of stress. Making changes and taking action can save you from complete burnout.

As stress is a serious metabolism crusher and sends so many people running for emotional eating, try these metabolism-boosting tips for your emotional wellbeing and to boost your metabolism to a high-performing level: These should become a regular part of your life:

Your anthem: Put on your favourite anthem and dance around your house now. If because of physical ailments you are not able to dance, then simply move slowly to it or enjoy it. Think how young children and even young teens love to dance when their favourite music video comes on TV. That freedom of spirit helps free you from stress and the dancing boosts your metabolism.

Handiwork: People carry so much tension in their arms and neck when stressed. Just carrying these clenched muscles around unsettles your metabolism. Try using your hands in relaxing ways to de-stress. Why not mix-up a batch of bread dough and enjoy the satisfying kneading sensation? Or buy modelling clay and savour the moment as you sculpt interesting shapes. How about taking turns with your partner, giving each other sensual massages with lovely, rich oils. All of these actions with your hands and arms continue your metabolism boosting and stress busting. Art therapy is used in many therapeutic settings to allow those struggling with difficulties to express themselves. It is no different for those looking to understand their emotions, as well as for you wanting to stop your emotional eating. Expressing yourself may have untold benefits.

Prioritise physical contact: Make physical affection a priority with your partner, including sex. This is a fantastic stress-buster and produces a number of feel-good hormones within your system that help equalise your metabolism.

Child's play: Child's play is great for you. From today, start reconnecting with things you loved as a child. Go on, have a swing on the swings in your park, rent your favourite childhood movie like 'The Sound of Music' or get out your favourite childhood game like Monopoly and play it again.

Let go and live a little: When was the last time you put your wellbeing above, for example, tidying the house? It's far better to let go of, say, being a neat freak and to go do something fun. Do you ever visit the funfair that comes to town in the spring or summer, or spend the day at your nearest theme park? Whizzing around on rides that are made for everyone (not just children) throws off the shackles of stress. This will invigorate your metabolism!

Calming days out: If funfairs aren't for you, do you make time to visit local special places of interest, or explore that farmer's market that occasionally comes to your town? Or go to the Christmas fair put on by a local church? A stroll around something that stimulates your senses in different ways is very de-stressing.

Life story: Keeping a journal is recommended for becoming more 'mindful' of your life and helping you identify and let go of stress. However, some find them a little boring, so why not turn your life into a novel? Write as if you were telling a story to a reader not just recording the basic facts of your day. Releasing your thoughts creatively is de-stressing.

Keep your stress radar running: Identifying potential issues and dealing with them as and when they arise so they don't build up is essential. If an inner voice tells you something's making you edgy then prepare to face it head on. Don't sweep things under the carpet as they simply pile up to unmanageable levels. I call this 'life's carpet bump'. How big is yours? Acknowledging stress helps tremendously with emotional eating because increasing your awareness of potential difficulties helps arm you to face the emotions surrounding them.

Learn to identify stressful thinking: If you're getting better at heading off stress (such as by following the tip above), but sometimes it slips through, learn to turn off irrational, stressful thoughts like, 'This [stressful event] is going to take it out of me'. It won't if you switch on a positive, confident inner voice telling you that you can cope.

Keep loved ones informed: If you're married/living with your partner, or living with family/friends or even roommates, it's important to flag up to them when you're heading for a stressful time, for example, at work, so you can both/all prepare for it.
Head off potential problems: If you've got a deadline looming that you're simply not going to meet then tell your manager. They'll appreciate your honesty even if they're annoyed. What's worse:

a little negativity from them or you harming your metabolism with excessive stress over the situation?

Develop the 'I can handle it' mentality: So what if your boss criticises you or your partner's unhappy you haven't managed to get through all the chores—can you cope with their negativity or are you going to let it cause you stress and drag down your energy and metabolism? As an emotional eater, previously you have been allowing such things to overwhelm you, but I hope now you're seeing that facing these things takes the sting and stress out.

As with the discussion on how to get a better night's sleep in the previous chapter, there are many similar practical steps to take to manage stress including: starting to say no to requests that take away from your relaxation time; stop using caffeine to pick you up and alcohol to relax you; get out for things like comedy evenings, films or other events—anything that takes your mind off stress. Switch off your negative inner voice that tells you you're useless, or a failure; don't let other people's criticisms and/or issues play on your mind. Keep reminding yourself that worrying about such things won't get you anywhere. Then manage your stress by setting goals to tackle such issues, put pen to paper and generate lots of possible solutions. If issues with your partner cause you stress, sit down together and take a fresh look at any troubles. Also, get practical. Set your alarm ten minutes earlier so you don't start the day rushing. Finally, it is very important to eat good, nourishing food that doesn't sap your metabolism. We now know that processed foods, things packed with sugar, fatty foods and other nutritionally-poor foods deplete your energy levels.

Over the years in my life-coaching work I've identified three main stress profiles. All of these upset your metabolism, deplete your energy and ability to handle your emotional life and, of course, may lead to emotional eating. Read through these and see if any resonate with you. All of the advice above applies to these profiles.

The Volcano:

This stress profile applies to those who carry a lot of anger within them. You're ready to explode at any time when things don't go your way, but often you keep it held in. Your anger may be justified, but you still find it hard to talk to people about issues. Your angry emotions cause you anxiety. When you do let rip you often do so at loved ones and not towards the person you have the issue with, like, for example, a colleague at work. Left unchecked your stress levels will keep on increasing and might cause you future problems.

The Hamster:

Like the hamster on the wheel you go round and round when faced with difficulties, finding it hard to look for solutions. You worry you don't want to be rejected if you raise issues with others that involve tricky emotions. Your stress profile means you get stressed but you tend not to face your 'stressors' head on, leaving you burdened with negative feelings. In the long term you're likely to suffer chronic anxiety and maybe even depression.

The Control Freak:

This stress profile means you rely on yourself completely, even when others could help. You overburden yourself trying to do things to the highest standards. Remember the perfectionist trait I described? This is you. You find it hard to let go. If you're not careful you'll be prone to exhaustion and illness due to your rising stress levels—plus lots of emotional eating.

LET'S CONTINUE METABOLISM BOOSTING

Having focused on stress as a big metabolism crusher, let's get practical and look at a variety of metabolism boosters. These range from the very easy to those needing a bit more time, effort and investment from you. As with all tips and techniques in the EED try as many as you can. Get that metabolism working for you so you can start seeing positive changes. Don't forget that energising your metabolism has payoffs with helping control your weight and giving you the energy to face the emotions that encourage you to emotionally eat.

As so many of us spend much of our time at work, I will start by exploring a number of energy boosters to try when at the office.

Steven's story illustrates how kick-starting your metabolism can kick-start a new feeling of optimism and fuel the desire to stop emotional eating.

Steven is a 42-year-old manager of an online business who found that boredom and being stuck at his desk for long hours left him feeling sluggish. Steven felt unmotivated because he knew his job inside out and, combined with feeling emotionally stagnant, he was emotionally eating.

Steven was more of a solitary person than a people person and found it hard to talk about his personal desire for self-improvement and his desire to engage in work that was more challenging. He was also having difficulties in his marriage. However, he and his wife were still very much in love and Steven was optimistic that this was the least of his problems.

In coaching, Steven focused on changing his feelings of boredom and the sluggishness it created. We discussed a number of techniques to kick-start his metabolism. With his quiet demeanour this seemed a good and practical place to start.

Steven immediately took to the very practical desk and office-bound tips that have been laid out below, and as he was in a private location at work he could put them into action. These tips energised his metabolism and encouraged him to want to take up a healthy pursuit outside of work. This was easier to put into action than it would be for some as Steven's wife was very active and he joined her on weekend hikes, as well as joining a walking club.

Steven's newfound sense of feeling energised made him think about his comfort eating and tackling its root cause: having felt unable to discuss finding a more challenging role at work. Steven also found that while hiking, he started opening up to his wife about wanting to do more with his life. He felt extremely positive about the changes he was making, which all started with becoming aware of the need to boost his metabolism.

It's incredible how implementing tips like the following can get you thinking about improving your well-being, opening up and facing previously tricky emotions—and ultimately kindling a desire to conquer emotional eating.

Here are some metabolism boosters to try that are essentially gentle exercise that you can do during your day. Exercise of any type will serve to speed up your heart rate and breathing and get your blood pumping. Even gentle boosters like these can put you in a better frame of mind with your body feeling mildly energised.

* Simply rotate your hands and feet vigorously every hour while seated at your desk. This action helps get your system flowing.
* Consider a workstation where you stand and can easily move back and forth from one foot to the other to get your circulation going.
* Stretch your arms upwards to the ceiling and do the 'seal', where you mimic clapping your hands together ten times. If you're on your own in your office, go ahead and clap loud and clear!
* Do regular bottom and thigh squeezes at your desk in repetitions of five. Squeeze tightly and hold for the count of five and then release. These can also be done on the sofa if you're watching television or if you use public transport when

you're sitting there on the train, bus or underground. That simple squeezing will improve your blood flow.

* When you have to go to the staff toilet, make it a brisk walk there and back as an energiser. While there, jiggle and jump (if you're physically able to) up and down five times to get your circulation pumping.

* Make taking the stairs at work—and everywhere—a daily habit.

* Get up and away from your desk as frequently as possible, as sedentary people who don't get up have a much slower metabolism. Even if you have nowhere to go it's all about energising yourself.

* Don't use the staff canteen. Instead, take a brisk walk to a local café to increase circulation.

* At home you can do fun things like skipping in place for a few minutes every time you feel your energy levels dip. There have been many times I've stood up from my desk while writing the EED for a few minutes of skipping.

* If you are lucky enough to have a large shower, stretch out your arms and circle them backwards and forwards a minimum of five times each.

* As you brush your teeth do a few gentle, slow squats and small lunges to give you a feeling of energy.

* Turn cooking in your kitchen into a bit of a ballet: swoop here, sachet there, twirl and lift your arms gracefully.

* Whenever you walk anywhere, walk with purpose! One study found that people who walk regularly and briskly were far healthier. They boost their metabolism in the most natural way possible. If you're a dog owner make sure you keep up with your pet pooch so you can boost both of your metabolisms.

* Start raising your metabolism with exercise that doesn't have to be a drudge. For instance, join a Latin American or ballroom dancing class. You don't have to be part of a

couple to do so as they are full of singles having fun. The musical element to dance classes is also a fantastic boost and the people I know who regularly dance seem to benefit fantastically. I also find dancing a tremendous boost. If you're part of a couple then get your partner to join you dancing—it might just rekindle any dormant romantic feelings.

* After you've worked up a sweat, why not share a steamy shower or bath together to unwind. Your body has had its work out—and that means your metabolism has had a little work out—and now you can start to enjoy some post-exercise relaxation. Unwinding in a bath or shower allows your metabolism to calm down after something like dancing. And if you're part of a couple, who knows where it might lead? Perhaps to some metabolism-boosting sex?

* Speaking of sex, why not plan a romantic weekend full of little surprises? Weekends away are fantastic metabolism boosters but they can be expensive, so why not recreate that feeling of anticipation in your own home? A weekend dedicated to each other invigorates your relationship as well as helping fire up your metabolism with the excitement. Or, alternatively, choose your moment for relationship and metabolism-boosting fun. For instance, surprise your partner with a romantic breakfast in bed. The fun and fizz of doing something different like this also connects you emotionally. When they arrive home from work, run a candlelit bath for them to relax in as you pour them a delicious drink. If you have children, arrange for them to stay at their grandparents' or with friends and slip into something new to seduce your partner in. Have a platter of finger foods ready to hand feed each other—of course making sure they're healthful foods! You'll both feel boosted with excitement, and these moments help open up better communication over any emotional issues you may have been keeping from your partner.

* A scary film or thriller is perfect for shaking up your metabolism. In the last chapter I mentioned not to watch anything too invigorating before bedtime, but you can take advantage of these on a weekend afternoon.
* You can get the same benefit from a thrill-seeking adventure like abseiling, rock climbing (many local gyms and community centres now have abseiling or rock climbing walls), white-water rafting or body boarding. These probably aren't things you can do very often, but even planning one special and thrilling event—perhaps for an occasion like a birthday or anniversary—will kick-start that fizzing feeling of your metabolism getting a healthy workout.
* Take up the ancient Oriental art of tai chi. The graceful movements help you in so many ways with your metabolism, your balance and with movement.
* There are many different varieties of yoga to suit every physical need. From the most gentle to the toughest workouts in super-heated gyms where you work up a big sweat, yoga keeps your joints flexible and your metabolism boosted and can bring you emotional equilibrium.
* Of course, you could always take up classic exercises like aerobics and gym work, tennis, swimming, running, bowling, hiking, cycling or boating. These exercises are all fantastic for invigorating yourself.
* Take yourself out of your comfort zone by doing something like an amateur dramatics class that can give you a real lift. Drama therapy is something people use to learn to express different emotions.
* Believe it or not, meditation actually promotes a good metabolism because it gives us the quiet time we all need to focus on the rhythm of our breathing, the beating of our hearts and the sense of our lifeblood moving throughout our body. Meditate in a quiet room wearing comfortable, loose clothing and focusing on a calming visualisation.

The above tips and techniques will help you keep your metabolism running at its optimal level. Many of them are natural metabolism, as well as mood, boosters. Think how good you're going to feel in both metabolism and mood if you strike out and go to a dance class? Of course, once you start to embrace the whole idea of metabolism boosting in your daily life I hope you'll devise your own methods to use.

Ultimately, the key word when thinking about your metabolism functioning at an optimal level is 'prevention'. You should be aware of keeping it at its peak to help keep you at your emotional and physical peak. Why not make a note in your PC, laptop, tablet or mobile of the boosters you're going to try over the coming weeks? Why not pop reminders in your diary on different days to try different ones?

At this point in the EED I'm sure you can see the holistic approach I have taken with your emotional wellbeing to help you prevent emotional eating. Armed with these metabolism boosters, I hope you find you are starting to get a whole new lease on your emotional life. It is important to remember that having energy to face your emotions means your emotions won't sap your energy.

CHAPTER 9

Appetite Management Tips, Tricks and Techniques

Small steps can lead to big changes when it comes to managing appetite

You've come a long way over the last eight chapters and you now possess much insight into your emotional eating. This insight will equip you to understand and face difficult or tricky emotions. I hope you realise you're now well on your way to tackling and preventing emotional eating.

They say 'knowledge is power', but self-knowledge is even more powerful as it gives you a solid foundation on which to move forward. Throughout the EED I've provided lots of advice already, ranging from the emotional—like how to identify the emotional triggers that send you to comfort eat—to the practical, like not shopping when hungry. Where relevant, I've included many practical tips, and this chapter is no different as it focuses on the key tips you can use in appetite management.

What follows is a truly unique selection of appetite management tips, tricks and techniques. These range from those that are easy and quick to apply to your life, to the quirky and to those with deeper psychological and emotional elements.

These work at different levels to help take the edge off of an appetite driven by emotions rather than an actual need to fuel your energy levels. For instance, some of them work to trick your mind into thinking it's getting a bigger portion of food than it is. Others work by giving you a subtle nudge to move on and not sit for long, preventing 'grazing': continuing to pick at food after a meal.

Start applying these to your life today and they will help you manage your appetite. Again, I want to remind you I'm not talking about restricting your food intake in unhealthy ways. As I've already explained, excessive or unnecessary food restriction and dieting are simply not good for you. Plus they ultimately lead to weight gain. The aim of the following advice is to help you with your impulses to emotionally eat, not to harm you in any way.

Some of these tips and techniques help to start shaping the mindset necessary to ignore some of your impulses to emotionally eat. It's important to think of these as enhancing your life rather than taking away from it. This isn't about depriving yourself of your favourite foods, because there's no reason you can't have occasional treats when you're managing the rest of your eating. Instead, these are about moderating the rest of your eating, keeping it balanced and to the levels you need to get through your day.

Have you been dieting up until this point? If, prior to starting the EED, you were on all sorts of diets, you may be suffering from what nutritionists call 'diet-exhaustion'. Diet exhaustion means your metabolism might be running at an unnatural level for you and you're undoubtedly physically and emotionally drained. If this is the case, and you've been on one diet after another before reading the EED, to make the most of these appetite management tips come back to them in two weeks' time after returning to your usual eating pattern. In the meantime, focus on getting to grips with the emotional and practical advice in the other chapters. This should give you time for your metabolism to settle down and mindset to find equilibrium.

THE POWER OF BEHAVIOURAL CHANGE

It is incredible how changes to your behaviour, and to your environment, can make a big difference to moderating your appetite. Combined with handling your emotions, you'll be successful at maintaining a healthy weight for life. Your motto might just become: 'change my behaviour and I'll change my emotional eating!'

Once you master your emotions and make behavioural changes, you will be far more motivated to follow a healthier eating plan. Together these will enhance your wellbeing and you'll begin to lose weight at a slow but steady pace—the best way.

Recent research can give you an idea of just how one behavioural change can make such a difference. One study found that by participants simply substituting a glass of water for each sugar-laden drink they normally had helped them lose 5 per cent of their body weight in six months. If this small behavioural change made such a difference to the participants' waistlines, it is definitely worth adopting the following behavioural tips to rein in unnecessary emotional eating.

TIPS, TRICKS AND TECHNIQUES

Cool blue: Serving food on plates of cool tones like mid-blue has been shown to help moderate appetite. Evidently, these mid-blue, cool shades like duck egg and sky blue help to switch off your hunger. If the budget does not permit buying a new set of plates and bowls then invest in one plate and a bowl in this shade. Then make sure you always eat from them.

Kitchen colours: Just as with your crockery, it may be worth painting your kitchen or dining area in cool blue too. Painting your kitchen in inviting shades means you may want to spend more time there, and that means you're more likely to pick up whatever's sitting around. It becomes far too easy to grab a biscuit or some leftovers without you even noticing. A cool blue is still an attractive colour but it's less welcoming than other warmer tones, so you may well spend less time in the kitchen. Of course, if you'd rather have a super-welcoming kitchen in warm colours like earth tones, then perhaps make a behavioural change instead in which you limit how long you can lounge your kitchen after meals. Also, clean up after meals straight away and put leftovers away so there are fewer temptations easy to pick at.

Sitting pretty: Staying in the dining area—don't buy chairs that are so comfortable you end up doing everything there, within hands-reach of lots of food. Even if you like to socialise and cook dinner for friends, once dinner is finished move into another area away from the tasty dishes that are probably still on the table. You may not even realise how often subconsciously you reach over, pick up the serving spoon and serve yourself a little bit more. Remember that food autopilot I mentioned that many emotional eaters develop?

Keep it hot: Research into body temperature has found that when you feel hotter it naturally switches off your appetite. So make the designated place you eat in your kitchen/diner also the hottest place. Perhaps the sun shines on a particular spot during the summer, or in winter perhaps sit next to the heater or radiator. However, don't take this to extremes and turn your kitchen into a sauna, as that will sap your metabolism. If being over-warm isn't your thing, the same result has been found for the exact opposite. If you eat in a colder temperature you will not want to sit there as long. So if you prefer you could keep your kitchen/diner temperature cooler, meaning you won't spend too long there and snack.

Form a good habit: When you have established your designated eating place, whether it is cooler or hotter, and with a less comfortable chair, then eat in this place as often as possible. This habit of sitting at the same place to have meals means you are far less likely to graze on the go.

Keep the good habits coming: I have already mentioned that sharing as many meals as possible with family and friends helps keep you emotionally connected. Feeling emotionally connected means you are probably becoming more skilled at communicating your emotional needs. Make it a habit to eat together as often as possible.

Mirror, mirror: Another extremely simple behavioural change that will help you with appetite management is to put a mirror up where you eat. A study found that when you're watching yourself eat you tend to eat much less.

TV snacking is a terrible idea: Ban eating in front of the TV, where, particularly if you're stressed, your mind switches off, leading you to then become engrossed in the programme and emotionally eat subconsciously.

Size matters: Hopefully you've armed yourself with a cool-blue coloured plate, but what is equally important is the size of the plate. You should eat from a smaller size plate for your main course and a larger size plate for salads and vegetables. When having your favourite foods it's far too easy to want to fill your plate with it. If you are eating from a smaller plate you can't fill it with too much, helping trick your brain into thinking you're eating your usual portion size. Give yourself bigger portions of salads and vegetables on larger plates. Of course, the vegetables shouldn't be fried or buttered.

Portion control: Try this little experiment: Serve up your normal-sized portion. Now remove one quarter of it and add in a glass of water with your normal mealtime beverage. This has been shown to work by making you feel just as full as if you had your regular-sized portion.

Miracle of mint: Evidently, something as simple as mint flavour helps control appetite. Try having mint tea between meals to help control snacking. Also, finish a meal with mint tea to stop those post-meal sweet or dessert cravings. If a snacking urge hits you between meals you can also try brushing your teeth—the minty-flavour toothpaste works, switching off appetite for some people.

Power of the pin-up: I have mentioned previously how photos from a happy time can give you a lift. When it comes to appetite management put up photos of yourself from a time when you were a healthy and happy weight. Of course, if you're 45, putting up a photo of yourself from age 15 sets an unreasonable expectation. Tape your happy and healthy photo to the fridge door so you catch sight of it when tempted to raid the fridge. Also, tape a copy of it to things like the biscuit tin—anything you raid when emotionally eating. Also, make this photo your mobile, tablet or laptop wallpaper and put it on your dressing table.

Take some 'selfies': This easy technique can be incredibly helpful in maintaining changes you make to put your wellbeing first, understanding your emotions and managing your emotional eating. Simply take a weekly photo of yourself to chart your progress. You should find you look increasingly happy, healthy and fit.

Shelve the cookbooks: One study found that thumbing through cookbooks with rich and tasty-looking photos of the recipes might just send you running for a snack. The beautiful photographs tap into a longing for food you may not have even wanted until the photos stimulated your appetite. Save browsing books until after you have had a good, healthful meal. You can then safely choose recipes to try at another time.

Picture this: In contrast, other research has shown that browsing through photos of certain foods does the opposite of what we would expect—it actually helps to switch off appetite. For instance, if you look at beautifully photographed salty nuts and then dip into a bowl of salty nuts you actually don't enjoy them as much and tend to eat fewer. This is because somehow the reality doesn't match up to the beautifully photographed commercial version. So, when you're tempted by those salted (and often fried) nuts, study the container photograph before allowing yourself a few.

Magic measures: When allowing yourself a treat because you're managing your emotional eating better, or perhaps you're having guests and you're going to prepare your favourite dessert for them, measure out your portion. It's far too easy to cut bigger portions of that fabulous cake you baked than you realise. Have a preset way for measuring various treats. For instance, I keep a little ramekin especially for measuring out portions of muesli to fuel my energy needs during the day.

Slow down: Slowing down the pace at which you chew food helps with managing portion control. This works because within about 15–20 minutes of starting to chew food, signals start going to your brain that you're probably satiated, that by now you have eaten enough for your appetite to switch off. If you've been quickly gobbling down a plateful of food you'll consume far more in that 15–20 minute window before your natural mechanism tells you to start slowing down. Eat slowly and you will eat less in that timeframe.

Keep it small: Cut up your food into small bite-sized chunks and it will help you reach a healthy weight. You're less likely to wolf your meal down because the simple action of cutting things slows you down naturally.

Musical influences: We know the power of music to lift us, move us or to get us to put on our dancing shoes and head for a night out. You can put this knowledge to use at mealtimes. Soothing music during mealtimes can calm any frazzled nerves, making you less likely to eat. Research into music found that playing slow tunes while eating slows down your eating pace. Put on some fast rock or pop tunes and your chewing rate will increase. Before mealtimes, however, use upbeat music to keep your mood lifted.

Get 'scent-ual': Evidently, you can stave off a craving for chocolate or sweets by sniffing a sweet scent like cocoa butter. So keep a tube of cocoa butter hand-cream in your bag or on your desk and it can kill two birds with one stone: making you less prone to snack and giving you softer skin. Although there are also fairly expensive scent patches available that you sniff when you get sweet cravings, this cheaper method can be just as effective.

The battle of the sexes: When it comes to reaching a healthy weight it is recommended that men go to male-only diet sessions. One study found that men had much greater success at losing weight when they could learn and discuss weight management with other men. Perhaps they were feeling shy about discussing their weight when women were around. So guys, if you're joining a weight-loss support group, you may well be better off with an all-male one.

Commercial weight-loss clubs: Although in the UK it's fantastic that you can participate in the NHS weight-loss service called the Size Down service, one study found people fared better joining commercial weight-loss clubs. Perhaps this is due to feeling that if you've paid for a commercial weight-loss club you're more invested in it.

Secret sugar: Beware of hidden sugars! Research by one professor in America found that eating foods with hidden sugars tends to set in motion a cycle of cravings. It is worth finding out the sugar content in your favourite foods, then you can swap them for similar foods with lower sugar levels.

Take a look at the labels: This simple behavioural change may have untold benefits. A study found that those people who take time to read the labels on foods when shopping are more likely to choose the healthy option. Make reading the labels and choosing the healthy option one of your good food habits.

Fake your faves: If you love rich cheddar cheese, try substituting with lower-fat but tasty edam cheese. Or if you love a decadent Mars bar, substitute instead a lighter-weight Flake bar. Research is on the side of snack lovers and shows that you can get going with weight loss by selecting the lower fat and sugar alternatives. Beware though that often the foods that claim to be lower fat also have higher sugar. So remember the tip above and check the labels when you're looking for better substitutions.

Chocolate heaven: A round of applause for researchers from the University of California who discovered those who eat regular (and moderate) amounts of good-quality dark or plain chocolate burn more calories. The emphasis is on dark or plain chocolate and not bars that are full of other rich things like caramel.

Go nutty: Research has shown that a small daily handful of raw nuts are enough to help with sustained weight loss. Walnuts, almonds and hazelnuts promote higher levels of the feel-good brain chemical serotonin and that in turn decreases feelings of hunger.

Boring meals: A study found that those who regularly eat the same meals lose weight more quickly because of food boredom. They are less likely to want second helpings of something they have all the time.

Sex-o'clock: Having a sex session burns calories, as well as releasing feel-good hormones like oxytocin and endorphins. Research shows sex may not burn as many calories as previously thought, but because it promotes these feel-good hormones and you are less likely to emotionally eat after a pleasurable climax.

Quirky exercise: I have already mentioned simple skipping as a metabolism booster, but make it official and buy a skipping rope. A few minutes of skipping helps stave off hunger pains, so keep it to hand and skip for a few minutes at a time when you start feeling an emotionally-based snack craving coming on.

Stick to your list: Shopping when hungry has already been written off as a bad idea. It's all too easy to grab a comforting snack in those situations. Also, try making your shopping list at home when you're not hungry as you're less likely to put snack foods on it. Make sure you stick to your list religiously when at the supermarket. Another simple suggestion is to simply make the snack aisles no-go areas.

Keep boredom at bay: We saw how Steven's boredom in the last chapter, coupled with other issues, led him to emotionally eat. Not only does boredom at work lead to far less job satisfaction but it also leads to more snacking. If you're feeling bored, then follow the suggestions I made in the previous chapter on metabolism boosting to get involved in on-the-job training in order to broaden your skills and gain more satisfaction in the workplace.

Wakey wakey: Since research shows early risers tend to be slimmer, you may want to set your alarm clock earlier—preferably getting up by 7 am. Early birds tended to have fewer depression and anxiety symptoms, as well as being more likely to eat breakfast. When you're feeling anxious or depressed you may well turn to emotional eating. Alternatively, many end up skipping breakfast because they are running late in the morning, making them likely to eat on the run, not to eat good food and to reach for comfort food as their stress levels rise. It's far better to have a proper breakfast to fuel your energy needs.

Lunch early, lunch well: It has been found that those who eat a late lunch find it harder to shed weight. Top teams at American and Spanish universities proposed it may be down to the way we process sugar differently depending on the time of day. Aim to have lunch between noon and 1.00 p.m. This ties in well with the breakfast tip above.

Packed lunches: To resist potentially high-fat, comfort-food-style offerings in your work canteen or cafes/restaurants near work, get in the habit of taking your own healthier choices that you pack the night before or first thing in the morning.

Budget for healthy eating: If it's difficult to pack your own lunches for work, only take into work the exact money you need to buy healthy options. By leaving spare cash and credit cards at home you can't give in to the urge to go buy comfort-food snacks.

Know the options: Always do a check of what's on offer at the canteen when you're not hungry and pre-select the healthy options. Research shows when you shop for groceries or go to a canteen/restaurant when very hungry, you're more likely to select high-fat foods.

Be vigilant later in the day: Psychologists have found that your willpower is more likely to break down later in the day, usually because of a build up of fatigue and the stresses of the day. If you're an emotional eater and you've been struggling to contain difficult feelings during the day, it becomes harder to resist comfort food. When tired, you're more likely to think, 'What the heck, I want a snack!' Recognising this can help you prevent excess snacking. As mentioned, some people's metabolisms run more efficiently on four or five snacks and meals during the day as opposed to three meals. If you're opting for more frequent, smaller meals, it's a very good idea to have a healthy snack or small meal already prepared for later in the day.

Sweet dreams: I have already covered getting a good night's sleep in chapter 7 when discussing boosting your mood to help combat emotional eating. I'll remind you that it's crucial to introduce a good bedtime routine, as studies find you're more likely to put on weight if you don't sleep well.

Body confidence: Since research shows that those who fret over their bodies are less likely to go to the gym, improve your body confidence by choosing the right gear. There are plenty of alternatives to the tight Lycra you may not want to wear. Find something comfortable and get going with some fantastic, metabolism-boosting exercise.

Choose your words carefully: Some quirky research found that when you are offered that extra slice of cake you are more likely to turn it down if you say 'I don't need it' rather than 'I can't', as in, 'I can't because it's going to spoil my diet'. Evidently, 'I don't need it' is more empowering to your willpower.

De-clutter: It's fascinating that those who have cluttered homes are likely to find weight loss more difficult. Psychologically, if there's chaos around you it may well be harder to keep track of how much you snack. It is well worth your time to spend a weekend or two de-cluttering. That is why many people get pleasure from spring-cleaning—it's a weight off your shoulders when things are more streamlined in your home.

Make exercise a mate-date: Exercising with friends has been shown to promote competition between you. You try that much harder and burn that many more calories—all good stuff for increasing your metabolism to burn calories quicker. So make exercise a friendly competition, giving you extra time with people you care about and getting fitter together.

Find a diet buddy: Experts have found that you're far more likely to reach a healthy weight if you're watching what you eat with a family member or friend. Enlist a person you trust to be motivated alongside you. This kind of emotional connection helps emotional communication, which leads to less emotional eating! Although some people will benefit more from the personal touch of enlisting a diet buddy, others may prefer to stick to the support of a weight-loss group.

Dining companions: Be ready to set your boundaries in line with the people you dine with. One study found that overweight friends sometimes encourage you to eat more with them. So prepare yourself to stick to portion sizes appropriate for your weight when with overweight friends. Or be ready to tactfully tell them to stop pushing you to have that extra portion.

Polish your plate: Dump the 'you must polish your plate' attitude towards food. The saying came from generations who had been through the Great Depression and World Wars, a time when it was crucial to finish everything on your plate and there was no room for wastage. It's obviously best not to put too much on your plate to begin with but if a host or hostess has piled your plate high with food you don't have to finish it.

Phone a friend: I keep mentioning the importance of creating and maintaining emotional connections. If you phone a friend or family member when feeling upset or unhappy, it will help you fight the urge to head for the biscuit tin. This is because so much of snacking is about getting comfort. Instead, 'hug' away unhappiness by connecting with a friend. Make it a motto to tell yourself that instead of having comfort food, you'll have a 'comfort conversation'.

Psych yourself up: Turning your emotional eating around will probably be easier if you spend a few weeks psyching yourself up by slowly reducing your intake of high calorie snack foods. Some research suggests a 'breaking in period' makes you mentally prepared for reducing comfort eating in the long run. So today, and on a set day each week over the coming weeks, drop one unhealthy snack or comfort food at a time. However, if you think that with your nature you need to go 'cold turkey' and cut out the unhealthy snacks entirely, just remove any snack/junk/comfort food from your cupboards.

One day at a time: Sticking with the psychological concept of making one change at a time, let's consider diet failure. People often fail at diets after only a short time because they are too future focused (and of course on a classic diet many fail anyway if they don't address their emotional life). When a diet is future-focused, the dieter looks into the future and sees their restrictive diet looming in front of them forever. This has the negative psychological effect of thinking you will always have to cut out favourite foods or treats. Always use a one-day-at-a-time mental outlook for appetite management.

Focus on your successes: Identify your successful 'off-button'. It is important to think about when you managed to resist snacking in the past. As with the things you record in your food and feelings diary, think about when you resisted emotional eating, how did you manage this and what were your thought processes?

One friend of mine, Hannah, 49, found focusing on the successful application of many of the tips and techniques turned her emotional eating around. In brief, Hannah had started emotionally eating after her divorce—it seems heartbreak has a lot to answer for when it comes to emotional eating. Knowing what an incredibly practical woman Hannah is, when we were having a heart-to-heart conversation one evening I suggested she try some of the above.

Hannah loved the fact that her natural inclination to manage things in a practical way could be put to good use, from everything to changing the colour of her kitchen and the temperature she kept it, to buying smaller-sized plates to eat on.

These types of tips, tricks and techniques made her feel incredibly positive and that helped her properly address the emotional pain she had been in after her divorce. I strongly advise you use as many of these as you can.

THINK YOURSELF THIN

Descartes said, 'I think, therefore I am', and I say, 'What I think I become'. Never underestimate the power of your thinking to guide your behaviour. Unfortunately, we underuse and underestimate our ability to think ourselves into various mood states and behaviours. You can so easily think yourself into a miserable mood if you focus on every bad thing that happened to you recently, refuse to see any small joys and happy moments that have crossed your path and moan about all of life's little woes. When you think like this you then behave in a corresponding way: your body language slumps, your facial expression looks miserable, you start saying negative things to other people and behave in negative self-defeating ways in the face of life's many challenges.

You also can think yourself into not losing weight by repeatedly sabotaging yourself, telling yourself you can't change and not having higher expectations for yourself and your behaviour.

Here are a few key cognitive strategies to help you think yourself to a healthy weight:

* Link negative food-related thoughts to sitting down. Each time a self-defeating thought comes to mind about tackling your emotional eating, sit down. Then take a moment to challenge that thought. For instance, if you've just thought, 'That stressful meeting with my boss this afternoon is going to defeat me, I can already see myself tucking into a packet

of biscuits', change it to, 'It's going to be stressful but I can manage it'. Imbed this thinking that you won't emotionally eat deep into your psyche.

* Next, stand up as you start imagining these positive ways of thinking. Standing up is literally physically uplifting. You want to feel that your positive thinking is literally uplifting you. Your thinking will then become linked to your behaviour.

* It is time to explore where your thinking has got you so far. Think back to the incalculable number of negative thoughts you have had and how they have brought you down. They haven't moved you forward over the years, emotionally. They haven't helped you with your emotional eating. Now that can start changing.

* Make your inner thinking a mantra along the lines of: 'I'm thinking of myself as a healthy weight—I'm imagining reaching that goal!" Put this mantra—or a similar one that works for you—into your mobile or tablet, somewhere you will see it regularly.

* Visualise what you will look like as you become happier by both tackling your emotions and becoming a healthier weight. Think about everything, from your strong, upright posture and wearing the clothes you want to wear, to seeing a smile on your face. Visualisations practised daily make a big difference to your thinking.

* Begin thinking about what new things you will do as you become healthy weight. Maybe you'll go to the gym more frequently because you'll want to show off your new workout clothes. Maybe you'll wear a more daring outfit going out to a party or event. Or it might be something more important like thinking you'll finally go out and look for that new job you've only dreamt about so far. Think through the details of these changes you will make because you'll feel so much better yourself.

* I now want you to lie back or sit comfortably and think about yourself as an emotionally-healthy person who is going to be a healthy weight. You are defining the new you from

today. Create in your mind that self-belief and commitment to positive thinking.

* To reinforce this new, 'functional' way of thinking, I'd like you to open it out and think about the last time you faced a crisis. What actually solved it? What coping skills were helpful? You probably found that eventually facing the problem and thinking through steps to manage it enabled you to solve it.

* Another simple technique to use is distraction. When you start thinking about, for example, how much weight you want to lose, distract yourself from that worrying thought. Immediately focus on something in your environment that will take your thinking in another direction.

* Initiate some fun thinking. Think about the last time you were laughing and sharing a moment with friends; the last time you had fun sex with your partner; or the last time you had done a good job on something. Retain that positive thinking as it will help you with the next emotional hurdle and help prevent emotional eating.

* Most importantly, think of The Emotional Eater's Diet as enhancing your life. You will have more energy, you will be in control, you will be thinking great thoughts about this diet that will change your life and weight for good.

From the content of your thinking, to what colour plates you should eat from, you're now armed with all the tips, tricks and techniques of appetite management. Together with all the other changes you're making in your emotional life, you're well on your way to a diet for life—a diet that looks after your heart, mind and body

CHAPTER 10

Embrace Your New Relationship with Eating

Understand yourself and you can now understand your emotional eating

We might have reached the end of the EED, but the next part of your journey to a happier, healthier life and weight continues. From here on in it's all about you putting to use every strategy and suggestion that you have read that is relevant to your life. I hope you will dip in and out of the EED for reminders on specific points and to help keep you focused on managing your emotional life.

I would like to highlight a key point from each chapter as reminders of some of the crucial concepts to keep in mind, but first answer the following questions honestly and see how much you've discovered about emotional eating.

1. Did you already realise that emotional eating can be on autopilot, and you might not even be aware that you're snacking?

                                         YES   NO

2. Had you known that certain personality traits can form part of your emotional eating profile?

                                         YES   NO

3. Were you previously honest with yourself that not facing your emotions could lead to emotional eating?

    YES   NO

4. Did you know in your heart that allowing stress to build up could lead to eating more comfort food, but still didn't change your reaction to stress?

    YES   NO

5. Were you aware that those who find it hard to face difficult emotions might end up in a love–hate relationship with food?

    YES   NO

6. Did you know that low self-esteem and the feeling that you can't stand up for yourself might lead to emotional eating?

    YES   NO

7. Had you realised that having problems in relationships might mean you head for comfort in food?

    YES   NO

8. Did you know that even the most apparently outgoing or confident person might struggle with insecurities inside?

    YES   NO

9. Did you understand how allowing work issues to pile up might lead to finding emotional release in eating?

    YES   NO

10. Had you realised that if you didn't set your boundaries you might end up overwhelmed and emotionally eating?

    YES   NO

Number of **YES** answers:_____
Number of **NO** answers:_____

You might have circled a lot of no answers, meaning that you hadn't previously thought about these links between emotions and eating before reading the EED. Your honesty is to be applauded and your new knowledge is to be celebrated.

You might, however, have circled many yes answers, indicating you already had this knowledge. Now you may realise that having that knowledge and not acting on it causes you to remain stuck in a pattern of emotional eating. This new understanding and fresh approach are fantastic insights to have.

KEY CHAPTER POINTS

I cannot possibly include all the major points from each chapter in this list, as the holistic approach to your emotional life and emotional eating covers a wealth of relevant things for you to consider. However, here are a few of the key thoughts that each chapter covered.

When writing chapter 1, I hoped to plant the seeds of awareness in you to consider how emotions left to fester or allowed to sweep you away can lead to emotional eating. Awareness is important because it serves as the springboard for taking action. By asking you to think back over all the diets you have tried and diet articles you have read I hoped you would ask yourself what was missing from each of those. Why hadn't they worked and why were you reading a new diet book? I hope that chapter 1 answered your question—that these diets had missed the important area of your emotions. You potentially followed these diets with a focus on one thing, like getting into your bikini, rather than a whole life plan.

In chapter 2, I wanted you to consider more deeply what we call personality—that wonderful, surprising, yet mystifyingly complicated way we view ourselves, how we present ourselves to the world, and how the world sees us. I highlighted how aspects of our personality can interplay with emotional eating. Particular attention was paid to three traits I have found that link a great deal of emotional eating: your confidence or your lack of it, your impulsivity versus how controlled you are, and your level of extroversion versus introversion. I described Emma's interesting example of how a parent's expectations for what they think your personality should be can be very destructive to your relationship with food. You may recall Emma's mother was very outgoing and expected Emma to have the same personality as her.

Next, I took a closer look at our emotions in chapter 3 and how not facing them, or accepting them, can lead to a pressure cooker situation. That means that somehow and somewhere those emotions have to be expressed—and with emotional eaters that's expressed through an unhealthy relationship with food. A key point was made about accepting that your emotions, especially difficult ones, are okay to have. It is how you respond to them that is important. One client, Helen, said it was like unlocking a key to a new life when she realised that if she faced her emotions they didn't take over. Prior to discussing her emotional eating, she simply felt awash with emotions that were out of control in her personal and working life. There is nothing to fear about your emotions—no matter how difficult they are—in fact a healthy regard for them is crucial to facing them. In turn this prevents emotional eating.

I hope that chapter 4 inspired you to start a food and feelings diary. This kind of nitty gritty, day-to-day information about what you're eating and why you're eating it can't be underestimated. A number of times I have mentioned the misconnection that emotional eaters have between mind and mouth. Keeping a food and feelings diary is a powerful tool to arm yourself with as you can see how this misconnection happens on a day-to-day basis. This helps you combat emotional eating.

Chapter 5 went deeper into your relationship with food. Crucially I want you to think how it can develop into a love–hate relationship with food not so dissimilar to having an addictive, passionate, love–hate romantic relationship. These damaging relationships can take over your life just as, left unmanaged, emotional eating can too. I hope this chapter revealed how this love–hate relationship can penetrate right into your heart and mind, get a grip and be hard to let go of.

A logical leap forward was to arm you in chapter 6 with lots of steps and strategies to feeling better about yourself. I highlighted how critical it is to overcome your emotional eating to feel good within yourself. Appreciating the wonderful you, respecting yourself and boosting your self-esteem equips you to face life and food and feelings in a positive way.

Carrying on this theme of empowering every aspect of the way you face life, chapter 7 focused on your mood and how to keep it lifted. One thing I have found with many emotional eaters is that they often feel in a low mood. This isn't necessarily as serious as clinical depression, but can be simply a feeling that their situation drags them down. Again, let me stress that you seek appropriate help if your relationship with food has become a battleground that might have led to real depression. I provided many different, wide-ranging strategies for lifting your mood. I hope they are the sort of mood boosters you have already put into action—from getting better quality sleep to enjoying sex, and a vast array of tips in between.

We got physical—and more—in chapter 8 to try and get your metabolism boosted. Letting emotion overpower you and propel you towards emotional eating plays havoc with your metabolism. Without a well-functioning metabolism it's much harder to change the way you relate to your emotions and emotional eating.

Many of you might have been waiting for chapter 9 and the tips, tricks and techniques to help you moderate your appetite. However, by placing this towards the end of the EED I hope you see how these can be incredibly helpful, but only when you are also managing your emotions.

I hope the wealth of ideas and insights in the EED have helped you to start embracing a new relationship with food. One of the biggest wishes I have for you is that you will now have many reasons to continue with the Emotional Eater's Diet, and that these reasons will keep you focused on continuing to improve your relationship with your emotions and with food. This is important because, believe me, people come up with all sorts of reasons why they won't stay on a diet, or in this case, a new way of relating to your emotional life and eating. In fact, the British Nutrition Foundation identified over a hundred main reasons why people stop doing a classic diet. They cited far-ranging reasons, from saying they gave up their diets because their friends are bad influences, to saying they are stuck at their desk and can't manage a proper eating routine and saying they can't get fit because they can only travel to work on public transport or by car and not do any walking.

What's my feeling about these excuses? You can create any excuse you want to not look after yourself, not address your emotions and not eat well. But ultimately you're only cheating yourself if you continue to allow your emotions to dictate your eating habits. Your motto should be: I will eat to fuel my body rather than fuel my negative emotions with food.

A final reminder that to keep motivated you need to keep believing you are worthy of facing difficult situations, standing up for yourself, doing what's right for you and finding self-respect. This takes courage especially if, you have never felt good enough to tell people when they are upsetting you or overstepping the mark. Part of the courage you need to continue on your new path is in reaching out when necessary. When you are feeling weak, as we all do at times, share those feelings with someone you care about and who cares about you.

This courage is also about forgiveness. You will at some point take steps backwards and you will have times of emotional eating, but you have to forgive yourself. Forgiveness means that you are allowing yourself to be human and not expecting yourself to live up to impossible expectations.

Keep remembering that food isn't your enemy. The 'enemy' is not facing up to situations and the emotions that go with them. Accepting you for who you are and believing that you're worthy of a 'diet' that helps you face life's ups and downs head on, will improve your emotional eating. It might also make it a thing of the past.

You may not realise it but you started a journey when you picked up the EED. Now you are equipped to continue on a better path. The misconnection between your mind and mouth that previously meant you used food to comfort difficult feelings is now evolving into a healthy connection between your mind and mouth. This healthy connection is where you enjoy food that nourishes and fuels your needs, as well as on social occasions.

I hate to say goodbye because I feel we've been on a journey together. But I'm wishing you the very best of luck moving forward.

Always remember:

Turn around your emotional life and you'll turn around your emotional eating.

Please make personal notes here

First published in 2014 by New Holland Publishers Pty Ltd
London • Sydney • Cape Town • Auckland

The Chandlery Unit 114 50 Westminster Bridge Road London SE1 7QY United
Kingdom
1/66 Gibbes Street Chatswood NSW 2067 Australia
Wembley Square First Floor Solan Road Gardens Cape Town 8001 South Africa
218 Lake Road Northcote Auckland New Zealand

www.newhollandpublishers.com

A record of this book is held at the British Library and the National Library of
Australia.

ISBN 9781742575100

Managing Director: Fiona Schultz
Publisher: Alan Whiticker
Project Editor: Emily Carryer
Production Director: Olga Dementiev
Printer: Toppan Leefung Printing Ltd

10 9 8 7 6 5 4 3 2 1

Keep up with New Holland Publishers on Facebook
www.facebook.com/NewHollandPublishers